Understanding Animal Abuse

Also by Clifton Flynn

Social Creatures: A Human and Animal Studies Reader

Understanding Animal Abuse

Clifton P. Flynn, Ph.D.

Lantern Publishing & Media • Brooklyn, NY

2021
Lantern Publishing & Media
128 Second Place
Brooklyn, NY 11231
www.lanternpm.org

This title was previously published by Booklight Inc.
(DBA Lantern Books). In December 2019, Booklight Inc.
transferred all its assets, including this book, to Lantern
Publishing & Media, a new company dedicated to the same
publishing mission as Lantern Books. Lantern Publishing
& Media's printing of this book remains the same as the
Lantern Books' version, unless otherwise indicated.

Printed in the United States of America

LIBRARY OF CONGRESS CATALOGING-IN-PUBLICATION DATA

Flynn, Clifton P.
Understanding animal abuse : a sociological analysis /
Clifton P. Flynn.
p. cm.
Includes bibliographical references.
ISBN 978-1-59056-339-7 (alk. paper) — ISBN 978-1-59056-
340-3 (ebook)
1. Animal welfare. I. Title.
HV4708.F596 2012
179'.3—dc23
                                            2011045101

CONTENTS

Introduction and Acknowledgments   VII

1. **Why Studying Animal Abuse Is Important**   1

   Defining Animal Abuse   2

   Why Violence to Animals Was Ignored   3

   Why Animal Abuse Must Receive Attention   4

2. **A Sociological Approach to Understanding Animal Abuse**   17

   Individual/Psychopathological vs. Social/Cultural Models of Violence and Abuse   17

   Social Structure and Animal Abuse   19

3. **The Connections between Animal Abuse and Human Violence**   33

   Family Violence   33

   Other Forms of Violence and Antisocial Behavior   40

4. **"The Link"**   47

   The Progression Thesis/Graduation Hypothesis   47

   Evaluating the Evidence for "the Link"   50

   Issues and Challenges for Future Research on the Link   54

5. **Explaining Animal Abuse: Theoretical Perspectives**   63

   Feminist Theories   63

   Symbolic Interactionism   65

   Combining the Two Approaches:
   A Feminist-Interactionist Explanation
   of Woman-Battering and Pet Abuse   75

   Agnew's Social-Psychological Theory
   of Animal Abuse   82

6. **Recommendations for Policy and Professionals**
   and Directions for Future Research   87

   Policy Recommendations   87

   Directions for Future Research   95

7. **Expanding the Sociological Imagination:**
   An Inclusive Sociology of Animal Abuse   109

   Conclusions   111

   References   113
   About the Author   131

INTRODUCTION AND ACKNOWLEDGMENTS

This book grew out of my work on animal abuse and its connection to human violence over the past fifteen years. Trained as a family sociologist, I spent the first part of my career primarily studying violence in families and intimate relationships. In 1996, my wife gave me a copy of Carol Adams' now classic book, *The Sexual Politics of Meat*, in which Adams so brilliantly presents the interconnections between the exploitation of women and other animals. This book led me to develop a concern for the ethical treatment of other animals in my personal life, and soon thereafter I gave up eating them. So it was only natural that I found a way to combine my new personal interest with my professional scholarship: I began to examine the relationship between animal abuse and family violence. As a bonus, I am now fortunate enough to call Carol Adams my friend.

This book is based largely on the work and writings I produced over the last decade and a half. In particular, significant parts of the following previously published articles and chapters, updated and adapted, form the core of this text and appear here in their current form with kind permission from:

National Council on Family Relations, "Why Family Professionals Can No Longer Ignore Violence toward Animals," in *Family Relations*, 2000, *49*, 87–95 (chapters 1, 2, and 6);

Purdue University Press, "A Sociological Analysis of

Animal Abuse" in F. R. Ascione (ed.). *International Handbook on Animal Abuse and Cruelty: Theory, Research and Application*, 2008, 155–74 (chapters 2, 5, and 6);

Brill Publishers, *Society & Animals,* "Acknowledging the 'Zoological Connection': A Sociological Analysis of Animal Cruelty," 2001, 9, 71–87. (chapters 2 and 6);

Sussex Academic Press, "Women-Battering, Pet Abuse, and Human–Animal Relationships," in A. Linzey (ed.), *The Link between Animal Abuse and Human Violence,* 2009, 116–25 (chapter 5); and

Springer Science+Business Media: Crime, Law and Social Change, "Examining the Links between Animal Abuse and Human Violence," 2011, 55, 453–68, Copyright © 2011, Springer Science+Business Media B.V. (chapters 3, 4, and 6).

I want to acknowledge all those who had a role in these articles and chapters, in particular the editors who kindly chose to publish them.

There are several people who have been respected and valued mentors to me along my journey in this exciting field of Human–Animal Studies. Ken Shapiro, Frank Ascione, Carol Adams, Andrew Linzey, Piers Beirne, David Nibert, Leslie Irvine, Hal Herzog, and Jan and Steve Alger have generously offered me support, advice, and opportunities to present my scholarship. You have been cherished friends and sounding boards for me and I am most grateful for those relationships. I would also like to thank Martin Rowe at Lantern Books, who took a chance on me with my first book, *Social Creatures*, and was willing to roll the dice a second time.

I extend a special thank-you to Piers Beirne, Leslie Irvine, Tracey Smith-Harris, and Lizabeth Zack for graciously reading an earlier version of the book and providing valuable feedback. And to Carolyn Gossett for the excellent job she did proofreading the manuscript.

And finally, I want to express my gratitude to my family for their love and support throughout this project and those that preceded it. To my two-legged children, Harrison and Clay, as well as my four-legged children, both living (Brett, Teddy, and Sara) and deceased (Maya, Bob, and Annabelle), thank you for your inspiration and for all that you have taught me about life.

1

Why Studying Animal Abuse Is Important

Until the last decade of the twentieth century, the abusive or cruel treatment of animals had received virtually no attention among academicians, particularly sociologists, criminologists, social workers, and family scholars. This was true despite its surprisingly common occurrence, its disturbing nature, and its negative consequences for both people and animals.

Most early studies in the late 1970s and 1980s were conducted using primarily clinical samples of troubled youth or violent prisoners. By and large, these researchers tended to employ an individualistic, psychopathological perspective, in which animal abuse was viewed as evidence of mental illness, part of a defective personality, and/or as a predictor of later criminality. Since this time, however, empirical studies of animal abuse, and its relation to other forms of violence toward humans, have increased dramatically not only in number, but in quality and stature. Sociologists, criminologists, social workers, psychologists, legal scholars, feminists, and others have recognized the myriad of reasons why animal abuse is worthy of serious scholarly focus.

In this chapter, after first defining animal abuse, we will consider the reasons that help explain why violence toward animals was relatively ignored for so long by both scholars and professionals. Then the case will be made for why animal abuse warrants attention from researchers, legal and mental health professionals, policy makers, and society.

DEFINING ANIMAL ABUSE

Deciding on a definition of animal abuse is a challenging yet important task. Depending on how it is defined, animal abuse could include the billions of animals who endure miserable conditions and deaths on factory farms each year or the millions who are suffer and die as part of scientific experiments. Other socially acceptable and legal forms of violence against animals, such as hunting, could also be included. Later in this text (chapter 6), many of the issues surrounding the definition of animal abuse will be addressed in greater depth. However, for this analysis, the focus will be on understanding the more direct and intentional acts of cruelty that are committed by *individuals or small groups*. Consequently, we will rely on the definition offered by Ascione (1993, p. 28): "socially unacceptable behavior that intentionally causes unnecessary pain, suffering, or distress to and/or death of an animal." Excluded from this definition are practices that are *legal and socially acceptable*, whether they are committed by individuals or institutions— such as hunting, animal experimentation, and factory farming. Also excluded are *unintentional* acts that have harmful consequences. Pain, suffering, and distress encompass *emotional or psychological pain* (e.g., teasing), as well as *physical pain*. And cruel behaviors could be acts of *omission* (e.g., withholding food and water) as well as *commission*.

WHY VIOLENCE TO ANIMALS WAS IGNORED

Why did scholars initially devote so little attention to animal abuse? Arluke and Luke (1997) have offered four reasons for this oversight:

- *First, society tends to value animals less than people.* Consequently, abusive or violent behavior toward animals is not taken as seriously. Arluke and Luke examined the prosecution of animal cruelty cases in Massachusetts from 1975–1996, finding that a conviction resulted in less than half of the cases, while only one-third of those found guilty were fined, only 10 percent received jail time, and counseling or community service was ordered even less frequently.

- *Second, other issues are seen as more important and are thus given higher priority by researchers.* Scholars and the public alike are much more likely to see matters like poverty and violence toward people as "real" social problems.

- *Third, because only a small fraction of the cases are ever reported in the media, public perception is that animal abuse is rare.* Again citing from the above study, only 5 percent of 268 prosecuted cases of animal cruelty were reported in the press.

- *Fourth, crimes against animals are seen as isolated*

incidents, committed by "sick" individuals, rather than actions that are linked to other behaviors such as violence against people, or to larger social and cultural factors.

In addition to these factors, I would add the following:

- *The extensive amount of socially acceptable forms of violence against animals (i.e., hunting and fishing, animal experimentation, meat-eating) is likely to contribute to an indifference about socially unacceptable forms of violence.* When this indifference to the systemic abuse of animals is supported by powerful institutions of religion, science, and government, and when those who speak up on behalf of animals are seen as overly emotional or irrational, then it is no wonder that scientists avoided studying this phenomenon for so long.

- *Finally, animals (and human infants) are the only victims of systematic discrimination and exploitation who truly cannot speak on their own behalf.* This silence makes it easier for all of us, including scholars and professionals, to ignore their plight and its relation to our lives.

WHY ANIMAL ABUSE MUST RECEIVE ATTENTION

In this section, I make the argument that the maltreatment of animals must be addressed for the following seven reasons (see Faver and Strand, 2008, for a similar argument addressed specifically to social workers):

- *Animal cruelty is a serious antisocial behavior that may help identify troubled youth and dysfunctional families.* Ignoring it may run the risk of promoting violence or not responding to psychological problems.

- *Animal abuse is a relatively common occurrence.* Studies suggest that half of all children have been exposed to it, and one-fifth have perpetrated it.

- *There are likely to be negative developmental consequences associated with harming animals.* Animal cruelty is a symptom of psychological conduct disorder, and might also lead to, or result from, an inhibition or distortion of empathy.

- *Animal cruelty can be a marker of family violence, as perpetrators are often victims of violence themselves.* Researchers have repeatedly found that woman-batterers often also abuse family pets.

- *Animal abuse is linked to a variety of other forms interpersonal violence, as well as nonviolent offenses.*

- *The number of potential victims is staggering.* When considering just companion animals, in the United States alone, nearly two-thirds of households have pets—approximately 160 million cats and dogs—and more homes have pets than children.

- *Ending animal abuse is an important step in ending all violence.*

Animal Maltreatment Is a Serious Antisocial Behavior

Violence to animals is a behavior, like other antisocial actions, that should concern parents, educators, clinicians, and policy makers because of the potential negative consequences it has for all members of society. Threatening to harm, harming, torturing, and killing animals are all unwarranted acts that deserve to be taken seriously. Among children, animal abuse has also been found to be related to other forms of antisocial behavior, including bullying and juvenile delinquency. (See chapter 3 for more on this relationship.)

Similar to other antisocial behaviors, animal cruelty perpetrators may be rewarded by their peers. Males, in particular, may use violence toward animals as a way to demonstrate their masculinity. Again, citing data from the above Massachusetts study of animal cruelty prosecution, about half of adolescent offenders committed their crimes in groups. Thus, parents who trivialize or minimize their children's actions, who fail to punish animal maltreatment or, even worse, encourage or demonstrate such cruelty (e.g., kicking the family dog, shooting strays) risk not only promoting violence and possible other antisocial behaviors in their children, but may also be ignoring their psychological problems as well as condoning (and sometimes modeling) their illegal behavior.

In the only known study to examine adults' animal cruelty using a national, representative sample, Vaughn and his colleagues analyzed data from the 2001–2002 National Epidemiologic Survey on Alcohol and Related Conditions (NESARC).

The NESARC survey is a nationally representative sample of 43,093 non-institutionalized U.S. residents aged eighteen years and older. The researchers compared individuals who reported a lifetime history of animal abuse with those who had never abused animals on thirty-one different antisocial behaviors. They found that individuals who reported a lifetime history of animal abuse were significantly more likely than those who did not to have committed *all* thirty-one antisocial behaviors. The most common behavior committed by someone who had been cruel to animals was doing something that one could be arrested for, irrespective of whether they were caught or not. The strongest relationships between antisocial behaviors and having committed animal cruelty were found for robbing or mugging another person, arson, and harassing and threatening someone.

Thus, violence toward animals by children, adolescents, and adults is clearly a problem that deserves to be taken seriously. Doing so will help to identify not just troubled youth and adult offenders, but also help the families and communities in which they reside.

Childhood Experience of Animal Cruelty Is Surprisingly Common

Despite the limited research, evidence suggests that the incidence of animal abuse in childhood is alarmingly high. Studies of college undergraduates from the Midwest (Miller and Knutson, 1997), the Southeast (Flynn, 1999a, 1999b), and the West (Henry, 2004) found that approximately half of the students had either perpetrated or witnessed animal cruelty, and nearly 20 percent had actually committed at least one act of animal abuse. These percentages might have been even higher, but the researchers used a measure that included only five of the most serious acts of cruelty: killing a pet, killing a wild or stray animal, hurting or torturing an animal to cause it pain, touching an animal sexually, and having sex with an animal.

In my sample of southeastern undergraduates, killing a stray and hurting or torturing an animal to tease it or cause it pain were the most common acts of abuse committed. As we shall see in the next chapter, males were much more likely to have been exposed to animal abuse than females. Two out of three male respondents had either witnessed or perpetrated abusive acts against animals, but this was true for only about 40 percent of females. The gender difference was even greater with regard to perpetrating abuse. Over one-third of the males (34.5 percent) had inflicted abuse on animals, compared with only 9.3 percent of females. Of those students who had been exposed to animal cruelty, three-fourths of females had only witnessed abuse, whereas one out of two males had actually committed animal cruelty.

Studies of schoolchildren reveal even higher rates of animal abuse. Baldry's (2003) study of Italian youth from nine to seventeen years of age discovered that over 60 percent had witnessed animal cruelty and half of all children had committed animal cruelty, with boys being twice as likely as girls to have done so. And in a later study involving children ages nine to twelve, two out of five had committed animal abuse, with boys again being more likely than girls to have harmed animals—46 percent vs. 36 percent. These rates are somewhat higher than those found among college students for at least two reasons. First, the instrument used with the schoolchildren included more subtle and less extreme forms of animal cruelty—asking if the child if she or he had ever bothered, hurt, tormented, been cruel to, or hit an animal. Second, younger children would have been reporting on more recent occasions of abuse, and thus, may be more likely to remember and report them.

Finally, in the only study using a nationally representative sample cited above (Vaughn et al., 2009), animal cruelty was measured using a single item: "In your entire life, did you ever hurt or be cruel to an animal or pet on purpose?" The researchers found a prevalence rate for animal cruelty of 1.8 percent. Although this number may sound small, if we extrapolate this figure to the approximately 215 million adults in the U.S. in 2002 (U.S. Census Bureau, 2006), then nearly 4 million adults may have perpetuated animal cruelty at some point during their lives.

In sum, as many as 40–60 percent of all children and two-thirds of male children may be exposed to cruelty to animals. Twenty to 50 percent of children and anywhere from one-third to two-thirds of male children may perpetrate it. Any behavior—particularly an antisocial, potentially harmful behavior—that is so prevalent should certainly receive the attention of scholars and professionals alike.

Potential Negative Developmental Consequences

In 1987, physical cruelty to animals was added to the list of symptoms that served as the criteria for the diagnosis of conduct disorder in the American Psychiatric Association's Diagnostic and Statistical Manual of Mental Disorders (DSM-III R), revised third edition (Ascione, 1993), and has been retained thereafter. The DSM-III R described the essential feature of conduct disorder as a "persistent pattern of conduct in which the basic rights of others and major age-appropriate societal norms or rules are violated" (American Psychiatric Association, 1987, p. 53). Physical violence and cruelty toward both people and animals are common: "The child may have no concern for the feelings, wishes, and well-being of others, as shown by callous behavior, and may lack appropriate feelings of guilt or remorse" (p. 53).

Since this designation, several studies involving children have linked animal abuse with conduct disorder (e.g., Guymer, Mellor, Luk, and Pearse, 2001; Luk, Staiger, Wong, and Mathai, 1999), along with other diagnoses, such as antisocial personality disorder (Gleyzer, Felthous, and Holzer, 2002). In the large-scale study of American adults cited above (Vaughn et al., 2009), having committed animal cruelty was significantly associated with a number of psychiatric disorders, including alcohol-use disorder, pathological gambling, conduct disorder, antisocial personality disorder, and several personality disorders (obsessive-compulsive, paranoid, and histrionic). The relationships were found even after controlling for a host of sociodemographic variables (sex, age, race, education, marital status, income region, and urban/rural residence).

One subtype of conduct disorder—displaying callous and unemotional traits—is particularly relevant to children's animal abuse and has received attention from researchers, as these traits may also be related to psychopathy and deficits in empathy (Ascione and Shapiro, 2009). A recent study of school-age children found that scores on a measure of callous-unemotional traits were positively related to committing animal abuse (Dadds et al., 2004).

Although several potential negative developmental outcomes could be associated with engaging in animal abuse, one in particular that has received considerable attention concerns the inhibition or distortion of empathy (Ascione, 1992, 1993). Inflicting cruelty on a smaller, less powerful creature may make it easier to disregard the feelings of other living beings, whether humans or animals. The inability to empathize with others may lead to treating others in a manner consistent with the above symptoms of conduct disorder—with callous disregard, and without feelings of regret or remorse. If animal abuse interferes with the development of empathy, then interactions with others may not only be unkind or unpleasant, but violent as well.

In addition to negative psychological consequences, exposure to animal abuse could also pose a threat to children's physical safety. In my sample of southeastern college students, one in five respondents (and three-fourths of those who had witnessed an animal being killed) had witnessed someone use a gun to kill an animal. Perpetrators were most likely to be friends or neighbors, followed by fathers, suggesting that either unsupervised gun use or access to guns (or both) may heighten the danger for children who observe animal abuse. Add to that the fact that half of respondents who killed a stray used a gun, and the opportunity for additional harm to the child or others becomes clear.

Animal Abuse May Be a Marker of Family Violence

Family violence research has consistently revealed that multiple forms of violence often co-occur in families. Thus it should come as no surprise that the presence of animal abuse in a family may also be an indicator that other forms of intimate violence, such as child abuse or partner abuse, are occurring. A recent study by DeGue and DeLillo (2009) demonstrates the association between animal abuse and family violence. In their study of 860 college students from three Western and Midwestern universities, 60 percent of students who had witnessed or committed childhood animal cruelty had also experienced either child maltreatment or interparental violence. Respondents who had been directly victimized—that is, sexually abused, physically abused, or neglected—were the most likely to report that they had abused animals. Further, students who had observed others abusing animals were eight times more likely than those who had not to have perpetrated it.

Interestingly, approximately 30 percent of those who experienced family violence also experienced animal abuse. Thus, the researchers concluded, animal abuse may be a more reliable marker of family violence than the reverse. The relationship between animal abuse and family violence will be discussed in much greater detail in chapter 3.

Childhood Animal Cruelty Is Related to Interpersonal Violence

Several studies have suggested a relationship between childhood animal abuse and interpersonal violence in childhood and as an adult. For example, violent prisoners have been found to have committed animal cruelty as children significantly more often than nonviolent prisoners or nonprisoners. Chapter 3 will examine the co-occurrence of animal abuse with other forms of violence, while chapter 4 is devoted to the specific question of whether animal cruelty leads to subsequent violence against humans. Thus, the presence of childhood animal cruelty may reveal not only information about a disturbed individual or about other forms of violence that might be occurring in families, but may also help to predict those individuals who are engaging in violence against others now or who may do so in the future.

If violence toward animals is related to committing interpersonal violence, it seems likely that it would be associated with approval of violence as well. Among my southeastern sample of undergraduates, students who reported abusing animals as children were more likely to approve of interpersonal violence in families (Flynn, 1999a). Students who had been cruel to animals had more favorable attitudes toward spanking children, even after controlling for frequency of childhood spanking, biblical literalism (belief that the Bible is the literal word of God), race, and gender. Further, respondents who had been abusive to animals as children were more likely to say they could imagine a situation in which they would approve of a husband slapping his wife. Given this association of animal cruelty and attitudes toward family violence, it should come as no surprise that violence to animals and violence in families often co-exist.

There Are Millions of Potential Victims— Including Companion Animals

According to the American Pet Products Association, 72.9 million households in the United States (62 percent) had one or more companion animal in 2010. This includes approximately 86 million cats and 78 million dogs (American Pet Products Association, 2011). Studies of companion animals have revealed that most people regard their pets as members of their family and many individuals develop strong emotional attachments to their animal companions (Albert and Bulcroft, 1988; Cain, 1983; Carlisle-Frank and Frank, 2006; Cohen, 2002; Siegel, 1993). In many instances, pets have been shown to be significant sources of affection and support for family members, especially during difficult periods and stressful life transitions, such as divorce and remarriage. At other times, however, such as when couples are making the transition to parenthood, pets may serve as an additional stressor, rather than as a source of affection and attachment (Albert and Bulcroft, 1988). Either way, parallels from family-violence literature would suggest that their status as family members may make companion animals more vulnerable to violence.

According to Walsh (2009), over three-fourths of children in the U.S. live with pets, which is more than the number living with both parents. Children in single-parent families have significantly stronger bonds with pets than those in two-parent families (Bodsworth and Coleman, 2001), and children without siblings report having the strongest attachments to their pets (Walsh, 2009). In their study of urban pet owners, Albert and Bulcroft (1988) found that pets were most likely to be acquired when families had school-age or teenage children. Perhaps not coincidentally, this corresponds to the ages when individuals first report witnessing or perpetrating animal cruelty.

Veevers (1985) first raised the notion almost three decades ago that animals in families might be at risk. In an article analyzing the roles of pets in families, she argued that one of their functions was to serve as surrogate enemies. In that role, the potential for violence against pets by family members was evident. Veevers posited that pets might be physically victimized as "scapegoats" or that they might be threatened or harmed as a means to control or emotionally abuse another family member. She also hypothesized that violence against companion animals could serve as a training ground for later interpersonal violence.

Ending Animal Abuse Is an Important
Step in Reducing All Violence

Information about why humans are abusive to animals is an essential element of any strategy aimed at ending all violence (Arluke and Luke, 1997). Ascione (1993) argues that the more we understand how violence toward animals is related to interpersonal violence in general, the more effective our prevention and intervention efforts are likely to be. Or, as Solot (1997) put it, "If we are to be successful in our quest for a society without violence, in which all living beings are treated with dignity and respect, we must have a better understanding of all types of violence. There is much work to be done" (p. 264).

Unlike any other form of violence, the published research on animal abuse has been motivated almost entirely by its association with violence against people (Arluke, 2002; Piper, 2003; Solot, 1997). Yet animal abuse, like all forms of interpersonal violence, is worthy of our attention in and of itself—not because it may be related to violence against others. Solot states:

> Even as we validate the connections among all forms of violence, we must take care not to invalidate each separate form. The woman who beats her children, the teen who rapes his girlfriend, and the adolescent who sets a cat on fire all need attention because they have committed horrific acts of violence against *other living beings* [italics added]—not because someday they might do something worse (Solot, 1997, p. 262).

Questions for Discussion

1. How would you define animal abuse?
2. Why might children who have been victims of child abuse hurt animals?
3. Do you think that violence to animals and people are related? Will ending violence to animals make the world safer? Why or why not?

2

A Sociological Approach to
Understanding Animal Abuse

INDIVIDUAL/PSYCHOPATHOLOGICAL
VS. SOCIAL/CULTURAL MODELS
OF VIOLENCE AND ABUSE

When scholars first began to research family violence in the 1960s and 1970s, most studies were undertaken employing primarily a psychiatric or psychopathological model. This orientation focused on characteristics of the individual to explain family violence, viewing wife or child abusers as mentally ill or "sick." Social factors, such as gender, age, social position, and societal attitudes and norms approving of violence in society and in families were seldom mentioned.

Yet as noted family violence scholars Murray Straus (1980) and Richard Gelles (1993, 1997) have pointed out, individual explanations, although appealing, are inadequate for explaining family violence. First, psychopathological models of family violence lead us to focus on the most extreme cases of abuse, causing perpetrators to be stereotyped as crazy, sadistic monsters, while ignoring others whose profiles and actions fail to match the pathological stereotype. Such a social construction of family violence enables us to "construct a problem that is perpetrated by 'people other than us'" (Gelles, 1993, p. 40). Second, the notion that abusers are mentally ill amounts to little more than a circular argument. The abuse itself is both the behavior that one is attempting to explain and, simultaneously, the factor serving as the explanation. (Q: "Why did he beat his wife? A: "He's crazy!" Q: "How do you know?" A: "He beat his wife!"). And third, clinicians have been unsuccessful in distinguishing abusers from non-abusers using psychological profiles alone. Straus (1980) estimated that only about 10 percent of abusive incidents can be explained by mental illness.

A similar pattern occurred in the beginning stages of research on animal cruelty (Arluke, 2002; Beirne, 1999; Flynn, 2001, 2008; Piper, 2003). Much like the early research on family violence in the 1960s and 1970s, the initial studies on animal cruelty also applied a psychiatric model, as researchers, often clinicians, viewed perpetrators as possessing defective personalities.

Such an approach continues to characterize much of the research on animal abuse. According to Arluke (2002, p. 405), "[U]ntil recently, understanding violence toward animals remained the sole province of psychologists and animal welfare advocates. Their approach sees animal abuse as an impulsive act that reflects psychopathological problems in the offender." Piper (2003) echoes this criticism, claiming that the explosion of research in recent years on the link between animal abuse and human violence has been "predominately psychological in orientation and is largely uncritical, starting from the premise that animal abuse is indicative of something pathological and more sinister" (p. 163). She goes on to say that an approach where this assumed connection is the dominant discourse limits our knowledge and understanding. Until fairly recently, then, the social context of animal abuse had been largely overlooked.

Just as with family violence, individual-level explanations for animal abuse are insufficient. Animal abuse is undoubtedly a social phenomenon, virtually always occurring in the context of human interaction and relationships. Whether animals are being threatened or harmed by batterers to control their intimate female partners; by children who themselves are victims of abuse from parents; or by male teens who are trying to prove their manhood, impress their peers, or express their anger at social or personal rejection—animal cruelty inevitably involves, and reveals much about, our relations with other humans. As will become clear in the next section, animal abuse cannot be fully understood by relying solely on the characteristics of individuals. Rather, social factors, including social institutions and cultural norms, all contribute significantly to our understanding of why people are cruel to animals.

SOCIAL STRUCTURE AND ANIMAL ABUSE

Gender

Gender is perhaps the most consistent factor related to animal abuse. Whether the data come from official records (e.g., Arluke and Luke, 1997; Coston and Protz, 1998), college undergraduates (e.g., Flynn, 1999b; Henry, 2004), school-age children (e.g., Baldry, 2003, 2005; Gullone and Robertson, 2008), or clinical samples (e.g., Ascione, Friedrich, Heath, and Hayashi, 2003), perpetrators are overwhelmingly male. This is true irrespective of age or nationality.

One exception is hoarding. Hoarding, a passive form of cruelty, consists of individuals keeping excessive numbers of neglected animals in poor conditions, which lead to poor health, starvation, behavioral problems, and death. It is estimated that at least three-fourths of all hoarders are female—typically middle-aged or older, single, widowed or divorced, and often living alone (Patronek, 1996, 2008).

In Arluke and Luke's (1997) study examining all animal cruelty cases prosecuted in Massachusetts between 1975 and 1996, 97 percent of the perpetrators were male. This finding fits with other criminological studies showing that crimes in general, and particularly violent crimes, are significantly more likely to be committed by males. Interestingly, the majority of complainants in these cases were female.

In studies involving college undergraduates, again males are significantly more likely than females to report having committed animal abuse in their childhood (Flynn, 1999a, 1999b; Henry, 2004; Miller and Knutson, 1997). Not only were male students more likely to have perpetrated animal abuse, they were also more likely to have witnessed it. In my study, males were nearly four times more likely to have committed animal abuse than females—34.5 percent vs. 9.3 percent. Two-thirds of males had either witnessed or committed animal cruelty, compared with 40 percent of females. Among females who had experienced animal abuse, three-fourths had only witnessed it; among the males, half had abused animals.

Henry (2004) found an even greater gender disparity in the perpetration of animal abuse. Using a similar measure, males reported childhood animal cruelty that was ten times that of female students—35.1 percent vs. 3.3 percent. Likewise, males were also more likely to have observed animal abuse—64.9 percent vs. 39.1 percent.

In studies of children and adolescents, abuse by males predominates. Baldry (2003) surveyed 1,392 Italian youth ages nine to seventeen, finding that boys committed two-thirds of the animal abuse. For all types of abuse assessed by Baldry (bothering, tormenting, harming, being cruel to, and hitting animals), boys were two to three times more likely to have engaged in abuse than girls. Similar results were found for adolescents in Australia (Gullone and Thompson, 2008).

How do we explain these gender differences in animal cruelty? It seems likely that both male socialization and the dominant position of males in society contribute to their abuse of animals. Boys' socialization involving masculinity includes lessons of dominance and aggression, while at the same time minimizes empathy. Combine these factors with a social structure in which men's dominant position in society enables them to more easily disregard the feelings of others and to use violence as a way to maintain dominance, and the high rate of male violence against both animals and humans should not be shocking.

Among the general population, women have significantly more favorable attitudes toward animal rights and animal welfare than do men (Herzog, Betchart, and Pittman, 1991; Peek, Bell, and Dunham, 1996; Pifer, 1996). This may be due to a variety of factors that encompass both female socialization and social structural influences. An orientation toward relationships, with an emphasis on empathy and caring, may cause women to broaden such an orientation to include animals. In addition, women's status as members of a subordinate group may lead them to oppose domination in all its forms, including human domination of animals (Peek, Bell, and Dunham, 1996).

Age

Like other forms of criminal behavior, late adolescence and early adulthood are typical ages for the perpetration of animal cruelty. In the Massachusetts study cited previously, the average age of all perpetrators was thirty. Slightly over one-fourth of the offenders were teenagers, and over half—56 percent—were under thirty (Arluke and Luke, 1997).

Arluke and Luke (1997) also found a relationship between age and the kind of animal abused, as well as the method of cruelty perpetrators employed. For adults, dogs were more likely victims and more likely to be shot. For adolescents, cats were more likely to be victimized, and beating was the most common method of abuse. Such variations probably are related to different age statuses. Since adult males have greater access to guns and may feel an obligation to protect their families and their property, dogs may be seen as more serious threats than cats. On the other hand, teenage males are more likely to commit expressive, rather than instrumental, violence. Thus, when inflicting harm is the intended purpose of the abuse, smaller animals, like cats, are more preferable targets.

In studies involving non-clinical samples of children, age is related to the perpetration of violence to animals. In the study of Italian school-age children ranging in age from nine to seventeen, older children were more likely to commit animal abuse than younger ones. In general, the rate of abuse increased as children moved from elementary school (10.4 to 28.1 percent) to middle school (13.8 to 36.9 percent) to high school (18.6 to 42.3 percent). Gullone and Robertson (2008) had a similar result in their study of Australian adolescents. However, these data could also indicate that, compared to younger children, older children have had more opportunity to abuse animals.

Socioeconomic Status

Like other forms of family violence, the abusive treatment of animals occurs at all socioeconomic levels. However, also like child abuse and wife abuse, the perpetrators of animal cruelty may be disproportionately represented among individuals of lower socioeconomic status. Munro (1999) makes this point from her perspective as a veterinarian in the United Kingdom. And Vaughn et al. (2009) found higher rates of lifetime animal cruelty among those with lower levels of annual household incomes (< $35,000).

In my sample of college students, respondents whose fathers failed to complete high school had rates of animal cruelty twice that of students with more educated fathers. Mothers' education, however, was unrelated to perpetration of animal cruelty as a child. When looking at fathers' occupational status (blue collar vs. white collar), students' rates of animal cruelty did not differ. However, respondents whose mothers were employed in blue-collar occupations were about twice as likely to have committed animal cruelty as children as those whose mothers either worked in white-collar jobs or were not employed.

Perhaps mothers' occupational status serves as an indicator of the overall socioeconomic status of the family, with mothers in blue-collar jobs more likely to be in lower-class families, where animal cruelty may be more common.

Childhood Socialization
Family Violence

Research has demonstrated that multiple forms of family violence often occur in families and that childhood experience with violence in the family is related to the use of violence as an adult (Gelles, 1997). As with violence against humans, children may learn to abuse animals partly because their socialization experience has included violence in the family. (See chapter 3 for a more complete discussion of this relationship.)

In the first study that examined the relationship between family violence and pet abuse, DeViney, Dickert, and Lockwood (1983) found that of New Jersey families identified by authorities as being involved in various forms of child abuse, 88 percent of those that perpetrated physical abuse also abused animals. Fathers were the abusers in two-thirds of the homes; in the remainder, the children were the abusers. As will be discussed in greater depth later on, subsequent research has discovered that children who are victims of violence, who experience interparental violence, and whose parents abuse animals are more likely to harm animals (Baldry, 2003, 2005; Henry, 2004; Thompson and Gullone, 2006).

Peer Group Influence

Peers are also major agents of socialization regarding animal abuse. In Baldry's (2003, 2005) research on Italian schoolchildren, students who had witnessed a peer's violence against an animal were more likely to engage in animal abuse than those who had not. Overall, the strongest predictors of a child's abuse of animals were violence against animals by their mothers and their peers.

Harming animals may also be a way that boys can display and prove their masculinity to their peers, thereby gaining their approval. In the Massachusetts study, juvenile offenders were much more likely than adult offenders to have committed animal abuse in the presence of others. Approximately half of minors (48 percent) abused animals in a group, whereas seven out of eight adult offenders committed animal cruelty alone (Arluke and Luke, 1997).

Power and Inequality

In our anthropocentric society, humans enjoy absolute power over other animals. As we have learned with other forms of violence, more powerful members of families and societies, typically male, are more likely to use violence against less powerful others, often women, children, and other animals. Like women and children, animal victims are obviously smaller than their human abusers. Perpetrators tend to select victims that are smaller and physically weaker compared to themselves—dogs, cats, and small animals (such as rabbits, birds, rodents, and reptiles) (Arluke and Luke, 1997; Coston and Protz, 1998; Flynn, 1999b). Smaller animals are not only easier to find, they are safer targets. Few offenders say they harmed animals because they were dangerous or had been attacked.

Because of this power imbalance—socially, legally, and

ethically—animals are often seen as not being worthy of moral consideration. Legally, animals are considered property, and rights of property owners will always triumph over those of property—a status making animals easy targets for abuse. Since humans determine the laws and norms regarding how animals are treated, which animals are worthy of legal protection, and when the maltreatment of animals is socially "acceptable" or "necessary," then humans' dominant status means that animal abuse is a low-risk act and abusers are not likely to be deterred from their harmful actions. Finally, animals are essentially the only victims of systematic discrimination and exploitation who truly cannot speak on their own behalf. Thus the superior physical, legal, and social status of humans contributes to the abuse of other animals.

Social Institutions
Family
Years of family-violence scholarship have revealed that the unique characteristics of families contribute to violence among family members (Gelles and Straus, 1988). In particular, high levels of interdependence, inequality, and privacy make it likely that assaults may occur within families, leading Gelles and Straus (1979) to refer to families as "violence-prone interaction settings."

As we have seen, U.S. households are more likely to contain companion animals than children, and homes with children are even more likely to have pets. Studies have consistently revealed that the vast majority of those who share their homes with other animals consider them to be members of the family (Albert and Bulcroft, 1988; Cain, 1983; Carlisle-

Frank and Frank, 2006; Cohen, 2002; Siegel, 1993). Unfortunately, because of their status as family members, pets may also be vulnerable to abuse. Stress experienced by families, including stress that might be caused by pets, may contribute to violence against other family members, including animals.

The Criminal Justice System

Although anti-cruelty legislation exists in all fifty states, these laws often do little to protect animals and likely have little deterrent effect (Arkow, 1999; Francione, 1996; Lacroix, 1999). These laws are ineffective in part because they were originally enacted not to protect animals, but to protect humans from other humans, and to do so while minimally interfering with property rights. Since animals have always been—and still are—considered property, they have no legal standing.

Additionally, the legal profession has been reluctant to legislate and enforce animal-cruelty laws for a number of reasons, including (a) society's ambivalent attitudes toward animals; (b) the difficulty in defining cruelty; (c) most violations are misdemeanors, and thus are not prosecuted aggressively; and (d) a lack of funding and personnel for enforcement, which has led states to delegate enforcement authority to humane organizations (Kruse, 2002; Lacroix, 1999).

In Massachusetts from 1975 to 1996, of the 268 cases of animal cruelty that were prosecuted, less than half resulted in a guilty verdict. Only one-third of those prosecuted were fined, 21 percent had to pay restitution, one-fifth were given probation, 10 percent went to jail, 10 percent were required to undergo counseling, and 7 percent were ordered to do community service (Arluke and Luke, 1997). The minimal nature of these sentences is even more distressing when one considers that these cases, because they were taken to trial, are likely to represent the most serious offenses.

Similar results were found for recent animal cruelty complaints in a North Carolina jurisdiction (Coston and Protz, 1998). Of the 958 complaints received in Charlotte/Mecklenburg County, North Carolina, in 1996, only 27 percent were unfounded. Of the remaining founded complaints, 75 percent had received at least one prior complaint, 15 percent had two prior complaints, and 10 percent had three to nine complaints. Yet only six cases resulted in an arrest—all involving animal fighting—and only one of those resulted in a trial where the defendant was found guilty and received prison time. The animal was impounded in only 5 percent of the cases, and rarely was a criminal summons issued. Most of the time, the police simply made suggestions, tried to educate the owner, conducted follow-up visits, or issued a warning.

In short, given weak laws that are infrequently prosecuted and the rare convictions that result in minimal sentences, it should come as no surprise that violence to animals occurs. This reality, combined with an historical legacy in America of honoring and protecting both family privacy and property rights, means that as long as animals are legally considered property, then whatever rights they might have will always be outweighed by the rights of human property owners, who all too often are also their abusers.

Evidence suggests that attitudes are changing and that animal cruelty may be taken more seriously. In recent years, there has been a shift to strengthen animal cruelty statutes, with many states elevating some acts of abuse from misdemeanors to felonies. As of 1995, fewer than ten states had passed felony-level animal cruelty legislation. But by 2000, the number had increased to thirty-one (Ascione and Lockwood, 2001), and as of August 2011, forty-seven states had enacted legislation raising some forms of animal cruelty to felonies.

Cultural Attitudes and Norms

One of the most consistent features of our attitudes toward other animals is inconsistency. Much of the world holds contradictory, conflicting, and paradoxical attitudes about animals (Arluke and Sanders, 1996; Rowan, 1992). For example, survey data suggest that while a majority of Americans believe that animals should live free of suffering and deserve moral consideration similar to human beings (e.g., Agnew, 1998), a majority also believe in and support the practices that cause the most pain and suffering to other animals—eating them for food and experimenting on them.

Western philosophical and religious traditions have historically reinforced a utilitarian view of other animals, constructing them as lesser objects to be exploited by "man" (Singer, 1990). The Judeo-Christian tradition argues that humans are superior to other animals and have "dominion" over them. Such an anthropocentric view helps to render and keep other animals powerless, making them more vulnerable to exploitation and abuse. Interestingly, a study of Christian denominations in Australia found members of more conservative denominations held less humane attitudes toward animals (Bowd and Bowd, 1989).

Western philosophical traditions, from Aristotle to Aquinas and peaking with Descartes, emphasize animals' lower status and lack of moral standing. This stance essentially removed animals from the moral community and was justified by pointing to abilities or traits that animals do not possess: the lack of a soul, the inability to reason or speak or feel pain. The Cartesian view, for example, holds that animals are simply machines incapable of feeling pain, and thus are not worthy of any moral consideration. The combined effect of the Judeo-Christian perspective and Cartesian dualism continues to influence the attitudes of individuals today, making it easier not only to dismiss or ignore animal suffering, but also perhaps easier to inflict it.

As noted previously, most of the practices that cause the greatest amount of harm to the greatest number of animals—factory farming, animal experimentation, product testing, hunting and trapping—are legal. These practices not only appear to have the support of most Americans, but equally importantly are supported ideologically and financially by powerful social institutions as religion, science, and the government. The result of the extensive amount of socially acceptable violence against animals other than humans may make unacceptable violence—animal abuse—more likely as well.

Finally, some animal abuse may result from cultural attitudes that are biased against particular species of animals. Cats, for example, are often victims of cultural prejudice. One study of sixteen aggressive criminals who had committed extensive and severe animal abuse as children found that cats were victimized more often and were subjected to a greater variety of abuses than any other type of animal (Felthous and Kellert, 1987).

Questions for Discussion

1. Why is it not enough to say that people who are cruel to animals are "sick" or "crazy"?
2. Can you think of other social factors that might be related to animal abuse?
3. Most people with companion animals think of them as members of the family. Explain how, in some cases, being considered "family" places pets at greater risk for being abused.

3

The Connections between Animal Abuse and Human Violence

There can be little doubt that animal abuse is often connected to other forms of interpersonal violence. This finding is now firmly established in the literature on both family violence and criminology. In this chapter, we will examine the co-occurrence of animal abuse, first with violence to children and women in families, and then with other types of interpersonal violence, including bullying, juvenile delinquency, and violent crimes.

FAMILY VIOLENCE

Prior to the 1990s, most of our knowledge about the relationship between animal cruelty and family violence came indirectly, through anecdotal evidence in the reports of wife abuse or child abuse (e.g., Gelles and Straus, 1988). Nearly two decades ago, Boat (1995) referred to the absence of research on the connection between violence to animals and violence toward children as an "ignored link" in the area of child abuse. Yet hidden in earlier studies of various forms of family violence is evidence for the occurrence of violence against companion and non-companion animals in relationships and families where physical and/or sexual violence has also occurred against: (a) female intimate partners, both in heterosexual (Browne, 1987; Dutton, 1992; Walker, 1979) and same-sex (Renzetti, 1992) couples; (b) children (DeViney et al., 1983); and (c) siblings (Wiehe, 1990). Relatedly, studies of sexual abuse victims in day-care settings also found that abusers have often threatened to harm or actually harmed pets as a way to intimidate, control, and ensure the silence of their victims (Faller, 1990; Finkelhor, Williams, and Burns, 1988).

Animal Abuse by Children and Family Violence

As with other forms of violence, childhood socialization that includes exposure to intimate violence has been found to be associated with childhood animal cruelty. The following variables have been identified as the leading predictors of children's animal abuse: (a) being a victim of physical or sexual abuse, (b) witnessing violence between one's parents, and (c) witnessing parents or peers harm animals (Baldry, 2003, 2005; Henry, 2004; Thompson and Gullone, 2006). In addition, being bullied and/or being a bully have also been linked to children's abuse of animals (Baldry, 2005; Gullone and Robertson, 2008; Henry and Sanders, 2007).

Baldry (2005) examined the role of exposure to domestic violence and violence toward animals in predicting children's animal abuse among a sample of nearly 1,400 Italian schoolchildren aged nine to seventeen. Among the 50 percent who had abused animals, almost all reported a greater exposure to domestic violence and animal abuse by parents and peers, compared to those who had never abused animals. This was particularly true for boys.

Baldry was also interested in finding out whether perpetrating animal cruelty differed for children who had been exposed to violence between their parents and who had been abused themselves (abused group), compared with children who had only been exposed to domestic violence (exposed-only group). For both groups, being male and observing peers abuse animals were the top predictors of children harming animals. However, for those in the abused group, the mothers' violence both against animals and the fathers were the next most important predictors. For the exposed-only group, violence toward animals by both mothers and fathers emerged as significant.

Observing Others Abuse Animals

Witnessing animal abuse has clearly emerged as an important predictor of committing it. In the previously cited DeGue and DeLillo (2009) study involving 860 college students, of the six different forms of child maltreatment and family violence that were used to predict perpetration of animal cruelty, only witnessing others abuse animals emerged as a significant factor.

Two recent Australian studies (Gullone and Robertson, 2008; Thompson and Gullone, 2006) found that adolescents who had witnessed animal cruelty were significantly more likely to have perpetrated it than teens who had not. In their study of 281 adolescents from twelve secondary schools, Thompson and Gullone (2006) found support for this relationship when the observed abuser was a parent, sibling, relative, or friend. However, those who witnessed a stranger commit animal abuse actually had *lower* levels of animal cruelty. The researchers concluded that children may identify with or model the behavior of someone who is close to them; but when the abuser is a stranger, children may be unwilling witnesses who are helpless to intervene. In the second study of 249 adolescents from three Australian secondary schools, witnessing animal abuse was once again found to be significantly related to having committed it. This was true even after controlling for age, sex, and family conflict (Gullone and Robertson, 2008).

The impact of observing others commit animal cruelty may differ on the basis of gender. In a study of undergraduates, Henry (2004) found that males who had witnessed childhood animal cruelty had *less* favorable attitudes toward animals than those who had not, whereas females who had seen others abuse animals had *more* favorable attitudes toward animals than those who had not. These findings, when combined with those above regarding witnessing someone who is close to the observer versus a stranger, could help explain the dynamics involved in this process. Perhaps males are more likely to observe those who are close to them—for example, father, peers—harm animals, and model this behavior, leading them to disregard the feelings of animals. Females, on the other hand, may be more likely to be unwilling observers when strangers commit animal cruelty, and thus may learn to empathize more readily with the animal victim.

To get a general measure of the psychological effect of experiencing animal cruelty, I asked the respondents in my study of undergraduates in the late 1990s how much witnessing or perpetrating animal cruelty bothered them at the time of the first incident and how much it bothers them now. Those students who witnessed cruelty were more likely to be affected than those who had perpetrated it. Seeing another person hurt or torture an animal had the most negative psychological impact, both at the time and currently. Eight out of nine students who had witnessed someone hurt or torture an animal reported being bothered some (39.5 percent) or a lot (48.8 percent) when the cruelty occurred, and nearly three out of four (73 percent) said they were still bothered now. Approximately 70 percent of those who saw someone kill an animal reported being bothered at the time, and slightly less than half said that the experience still bothered them.

The pattern for perpetrating animal cruelty was somewhat different. Approximately half of those who either killed a stray or hurt or tortured an animal were bothered by their actions, both then and at the time of the study. However, those who hurt or tortured animals appear to be affected more later by their cruelty than they were at the time. Slightly fewer than 40 percent reported being bothered at the time, but 56.5 percent said their actions bother them now. Forty percent of those who killed or hurt/tortured animals claim that they were not bothered by their abuse at either time.

It seems clear that for a significant number of respondents, experiencing animal cruelty, and particularly witnessing it, resulted in some psychological or emotional strain not only at the time of the cruelty, but several years later as well. Why would the effects be more pronounced for those who witnessed violence to animals in childhood than for those who actually perpetrated it?

Several overlapping explanations are plausible. First, children who engage in animal cruelty are likely to have certain characteristics that lead them to be less affected by violence (i.e., predominantly males whose socialization has included violence). Additionally, committing an act of cruelty against an animal may create the need to justify that action by redefining it as something other than cruelty (like some of the students in Arluke's [2002] study described, which will be treated in chapter 5). Finally, one who witnesses animal cruelty has no control over the act; in fact, in some cases the cruelty may have been employed to shock, intimidate, or exert control over the observer. Witnessing the abuse and being helpless to prevent it may make the psychological impact even worse.

Pet Abuse and Woman-Battering

Several studies have now clearly established a connection between pet abuse and woman-battering (Ascione, 1993; Ascione et al., 2007; Faver and Strand, 2003, 2007; Fitzgerald, 2005, 2007; Flynn, 2000a, 2000c; Strand and Faver, 2005). According to the data, anywhere from one-half to three-fourths of battered women with pets report that their companion animals have been threatened, harmed, or killed by their abusers. These findings have been confirmed in studies involving women from different ethnic groups (e.g., Hispanics—Faver and Cavazos, 2007), as well as from other cultures (e.g., Australia—Volant et al., 2008).

Most studies involving clients from battered women's shelters have failed to use a control group. However, a recent study by Ascione et al. (2007) did employ a comparison group of nonshelter women from the community. Battered women were eleven times more likely to report that their pets had been threatened or abused than a sample of community women—54 percent vs. 5 percent.

These findings were recently replicated by researchers in Australia (Volant et al., 2008). Women who were receiving services from either a shelter or outreach agency serving battered women who owned at least one pet during their violent relationship were compared with a group of nonbattered women who were recruited from neighborhood houses, workplaces, and leisure and recreational groups. Slightly over half (52.9 percent) of domestic violence victims reported pet abuse compared with none from the nondomestic violence group. Threats of pet abuse were approximately eight times greater—46 percent versus 5.8 percent—among women in the domestic-violence group.

The first controlled study to examine the association between pet abuse and woman-battering was conducted by Walton-Moss et al. (2005). The sample of over 800 women was selected from the control group from a study of intimate-partner homicide from eleven metropolitan cities in the United States between 1994 and 2000. Women who had experienced abuse in the previous two years were compared to a control group of nonabused women from the same metropolitan area who were identified by random-digit dialing. In addition to being more likely to be high-school dropouts, have a problem with drugs or alcohol, and be in fair or poor mental health, perpetrators of intimate-partner violence were also significantly more likely to have abused or threatened pets.

Researchers have also found that most battered women consider their companion animals to be important sources of emotional support. This is particularly true for women whose pets were abused and for women who did not have children (Flynn, 2000a). These two factors may also explain why battered women are slow to leave these relationships. Studies show that approximately 20 percent of the women delayed leaving due to their concern about the safety of their companion animals. A woman was even more likely to put off leaving her batterer if the latter had also abused her pet (Ascione et al., 2007; Flynn, 2000c). And women with no children were more likely than women with children to delay seeking shelter (Ascione et al., 2007; Faver and Strand, 2003).

Abuse of women and pets also harms the children who witness these acts. Ascione and his colleagues (2007) found that 61.5 percent of the children of women at the shelters had witnessed pet abuse, compared with just 2.9 percent of children of nonshelter women. Similar results were found in the Australian study reviewed above—29 percent versus 0 percent (Volant et al., 2008). And both of these studies uncovered high rates of animal abuse among the children of battered women (13–19 percent). According to Ascione at al. (2007), this is three to five times the rate found in normative samples, and closer to the rates found in abused children or those from clinical settings.

OTHER FORMS OF VIOLENCE
AND ANTISOCIAL BEHAVIOR

In addition to family violence, animal cruelty is associated with other forms of interpersonal violence and antisocial behavior, including bullying, juvenile delinquency, and adult criminality involving both violent and nonviolent actions.

Bullying

Evidence from recent studies suggests that youth involved in bullying—both as perpetrators and victims—are more likely to abuse animals (Baldry, 2005; Gullone and Robertson, 2008; Henry and Sanders, 2007). This relationship appears to be particularly true for males. In her study of over five hundred Italian youths ages nine to twelve, Baldry (2005) found that both boys and girls who engaged in direct bullying were twice as likely to have abused animals compared with their nonbullying peers. Separate analyses were conducted for each gender, with six different family violence variables (exposure to father's or mother's interpersonal violence, father's or mother's physical and verbal child abuse) included along with witnessing animal abuse and experience with bullying (direct or indirect at school), either as victim or perpetrator, as possible predictors of committing animal abuse.

For boys, the top predictor of animal abuse was being bullied at school, followed by their own indirect bullying of others. Interestingly, none of the measures of exposure to various forms of family violence was significant. For girls, however, none of the bullying variables emerged as significant. The strongest predictor of their animal abuse was observing others abuse animals, followed by father's verbal abuse. And girls who were physically abused by their fathers were actually less likely to harm animals.

Henry and Sanders (2007) also examined the relationship between bullying and animal abuse among male undergraduates. In particular, they were interested in comparing those who had committed multiple acts of animal abuse with those who were one-time abusers and non-abusers. Those who had been involved in multiple episodes of animal cruelty were significantly more likely to have *both* been a bully *and* to have been bullied (both physically and verbally) than either one-time abusers or those who had never abused animals. A subsequent analysis to predict committing multiple acts of animal abuse contained four bullying variables (perpetrator and victim of physical and verbal bullying) and an attitudinal variable measuring tolerance of cruelty to animals. Only physically bullying others emerged as a significant predictor. Interestingly, male students who were both serious bullies and victims of bullying held the most tolerant attitudes toward animal cruelty.

Animal abuse has also been investigated as a predictor of bullying. Gullone and Robertson (2008) surveyed 249 adolescents in Australia whose mean age was just under fourteen. Approximately three in ten students had experienced bullying at least once in the past year, and nearly one in five had bullied someone at least once in the past year. Controlling for age, sex, and family conflict (none of which was significant), witnessing animal abuse (along with being a victim of bullying) was found to be a significant predictor of being a bully.

Taken together, these findings suggest that gender, power, and control are central to understanding the relationship between bullying and animal abuse. Those who abuse animals and bully others, especially males, appear to be rewarded by the power they have over others—human or animal. And those who have been bullied may want to transform the powerlessness they feel as victims by victimizing others—again, both human and animal. As Henry and Sanders noted, "Children who are victimized may feel the need to exert power over other weaker individuals in an effort to protect themselves from the fear and shame resulting from their own perceived weakness" (2007, p. 123). Later we shall see these same variables—gender, power, and control—help us understand men's woman-battering and pet abuse (chapter 5), as well as the link between animal cruelty and extremely violent male criminals (chapter 4).

Juvenile Delinquency

In two separate studies, Henry (2004a, 2004b) examined the relationship between animal cruelty and juvenile delinquency among college students. In the first study involving 169 undergraduates (2004b), Henry found that both witnessing and perpetrating animal abuse were related to committing delinquency—both in the previous year and ever. Among male students, the effects of participating in and observing animal cruelty were both independent and additive. So while observing and committing animal abuse were each separately related to juvenile delinquency, males who had both witnessed and perpetrated animal abuse on multiple occasions had the highest delinquency scores.

In the second study, Henry (2004a) looked at two factors hypothesized to be related to juvenile delinquency—the age of first exposure to animal abuse and whether animal abuse was committed alone or in a group. With regard to age of first exposure, males who first experienced animal abuse before age twelve had higher self-reported delinquency scores than those who witnessed it as teens or not at all. The findings for females, however, were not significant.

Since so few females participated in animal cruelty, the effect of perpetrating animal abuse alone or in a group was only analyzed for males. Males who had committed animal cruelty alone had significantly higher delinquency scores than those who had never abused animals. So, at least for males, exposure to animal abuse at an early age and committing it alone may be warning signs for other forms of antisocial behavior.

Violence and Other Criminality

A study by the Chicago Police Department analyzed the arrest data for people charged with crimes against animals for the period of July 2001 to July 2004. Those individuals who had committed animal cruelty were also likely to have committed other offenses, both violent and nonviolent. Eighty-six percent of animal offenders had multiple arrests in their past, 70 percent had been arrested for felonies, and 70 percent had been charged with narcotics use. Approximately two-thirds had been arrested for battery-related violent-offense charges—that is, aggravated domestic battery, domestic battery, aggravated battery, and simple battery—and over half were alleged to be members of gangs (Randour and Hardiman, 2007). In a more rigorously designed study which will be discussed more fully in the next chapter, Arluke and his colleagues (Arluke et al., 1999) found that individuals who had been convicted of animal abuse were significantly more likely to have a criminal record and to have committed both violent and property crimes.

Questions for Discussion

1. Witnessing other people harm animals has consistently been found to be related to perpetrating animal abuse. What might explain this relationship?

2. Having been a victim of bullying is a predictor of being cruel to animals. What might explain this finding?
3. Some studies suggest that, at least for males, exposure to animal abuse at an early age and committing it alone are related to juvenile delinquency. Why might this be the case?

4

"The Link"

Thus far, the discussion has focused on the association between animal abuse and human violence, without specifying a time-ordered sequence. In this chapter, we will examine the evidence for what has been termed "the link"—a more specific prediction about the relationship between these two variables. According to this hypothesis, individuals begin, typically in childhood, by abusing animals, and then move on to commit violence against humans.

THE PROGRESSION THESIS/
GRADUATION HYPOTHESIS

The Early Studies

Evidence in support of the progression thesis (Beirne, 2004) or graduation hypothesis (Arluke et al., 1999) has typically come from retrospective studies using samples of violent criminals—serial killers, rapists, child molesters—who report animal cruelty committed during their childhood. The first study of this kind (Kellert and Felthous, 1985) compared the extent of childhood animal abuse between criminals and noncriminals. The criminals were classified based on prison counselors' observations and their own self-reports as aggressive, moderately aggressive, or nonaggressive. Kellert and Felthous found that aggressive criminals reported significantly more incidents of childhood animal cruelty—and more severe acts of cruelty—than any of the other groups. One-fourth of aggressive criminals reported committing five or more acts of animal abuse as a child. This compared with only 6 percent of moderately aggressive and nonaggressive criminals and zero percent for noncriminals.

A later study by Lockwood and Church (1998) found that 36 percent of serial murderers reported killing and torturing animals in childhood, while 46 percent did so as adolescents. Perpetrators of sexually aggressive crimes have also reported relatively high levels of animal cruelty in their backgrounds. In one study, nearly half of rapists and over one-fourth of pedophiles had harmed animals as children (Tingle et al., 1986).

More Recent Studies

More recently, a study of 354 serial killers found that 21 percent had committed childhood animal cruelty (Wright and Tinsley, 2003). And in a study of eleven perpetrators of nine separate incidents of school shootings in the United States, five of the eleven had histories of alleged violence against animals (Verlinden, Hersen, and Thomas, 2001).

In a test of the graduation hypothesis, Merz-Perez, Heide, and Silverman (2001; 2004) interviewed forty-five violent and forty-five nonviolent inmates in a Florida maximum-security prison, asking about animal abuse committed during their childhoods. Violent criminals were nearly three times more likely than nonviolent criminals to have committed childhood animal cruelty—56 versus 20 percent. This relationship was particularly strong for pets, with violent offenders being nearly four times more likely than their nonviolent counter-parts—26 versus 7 percent—to report having abused their pets as children. Beyond these findings, there was also a link between the methods of animal cruelty and adult violence. Inmates' past acts of animal cruelty often resembled their most serious crimes against humans.

In another study, Arluke and his colleagues compared the criminal records of 153 convicted animal abusers with a control group of 153 nonabusers, who were matched based on the factors of sex, age, socioeconomic status, and street or neighborhood (Arluke, Levin, Luke, and Ascione, 1999). Animal abusers were over three times more likely to have a criminal record, and over five times more likely to have committed a violent crime. However, there was no specific time order to this relationship; animal abuse was just as likely to follow the violent offenses as precede them. Only 16 percent of animal abusers "graduated" to committing violence against human victims. Beyond this, animal abuse was also related to a variety of nonviolent crimes, including property crimes, drug-related crimes, and disorderly behavior. Thus, the authors concluded that this evidence is more consistent with what they termed a "generalized deviance hypothesis" rather than a graduation hypothesis. They posited, "Rather than being a predictor or a distinct step in the development of increasingly criminal or violent behavior, animal abuse . . . is one of many antisocial behaviors committed by individuals in society . . . " (Arluke et al., 1999, p. 969).

A recent study in Australia tested and found support for both hypotheses. Alys, Wilson, Clarke, and Toman (2009) compared twenty incarcerated male sexual-homicide offenders, twenty male sex offenders (who did not kill) from an out-patient treatment program, and twenty male college students. The groups, who were matched for age, were asked about childhood and adolescent animal cruelty, antisocial behavior (e.g., stealing, destroying property, and cruelty to children), child abuse, and paternal alcoholism.

In support of the graduation hypothesis, sexual homicide offenders were significantly more likely to have committed animal abuse, both during childhood and adolescence, than the sex offenders and controls. Interestingly, virtually all of the homicide offenders reported abusing animals, while none of the sex offenders did. Sexual homicide offenders also reported significantly more frequent animal cruelty than did the controls, both as children and as teens. Additionally, childhood animal cruelty was also a significant predictor for adolescent antisocial behavior for both groups; in fact, the relationship was stronger for controls than for sexual homicide offenders.

Yet support was also found for the deviance-generalization hypothesis. Antisocial behavior in childhood emerged as a significant predictor of childhood animal cruelty, and the same pattern was found for adolescence. The relationship was particularly strong for the younger age group. Thus the question remains open. As the authors assert, neither hypothesis can be dismissed.

EVALUATING THE EVIDENCE FOR "THE LINK"

Critics of research supporting "the link" contend that it is methodologically and theoretically flawed in multiple ways

(Arluke, 2002; Beirne, 2004, 2009; Pagani, Robustelli, and Ascione, 2010; Patterson-Kane and Piper, 2009; Piper, 2003). The major methodological criticisms are:

- *Most research is retrospective, or as Beirne (2004) puts it, "backward looking."* As a result, claims about whether animal abuse in the past is causally linked to later human violence cannot be made with confidence.

- *Much of the research is correlational in nature*, often making it difficult to determine which came first— the animal abuse or the violence against humans. It is also possible that both forms of violence are the result of some third factor, rather than being causally related to each other.

- *In most cases, studies employ samples that are not representative of the population as a whole*—typically, incarcerated criminals. Further, such inmates may have incentives to exaggerate their past violence against animals in order to enhance or reinforce their persona as "tough guys," thereby further obscuring the data.

- *The studies employ vague and inconsistent definitions of animal abuse.*

Likewise, there are conceptual or theoretical objections to "link" research, which include the following:

- *There are multiple pathways that lead to and from and through animal abuse.* Piper (2003) argues that the dominant discourse of the link closes off other ways of conceptualizing and theorizing about other causes and pathways of animal abuse.

- *Most who abuse animals don't go on to be violent toward humans,* so overemphasizing this relationship may lead authorities to falsely label and stigmatize children as potential abusers or worse, resulting in greater deviance, not less.

- *Research on the link has been overly psychological in nature*, assuming that the animal abuse is pathological. It has ignored the numerous social and cultural factors that contribute to the perpetation of violence against animals, much in the same way that early family-violence researchers focused almost exclusively on characteristics of the individuals involved (Arluke, 2002; Flynn, 2001, 2008).

These flaws led Piper (2003) to refer to research on the linkage of animal abuse with interpersonal violence as a "sheep in wolf's clothing."

Yet there are also problems associated with the Arluke et al. (1999) study, which prevent it from refuting the graduation/progression thesis.

- *The study relied on official crime records.* Since these

records contain only reported crime, earlier animal-cruelty crimes would not be included.

- *Only adult criminals were included*, as the researchers were not able to obtain the records of juvenile offenders (ages sixteen and under). Therefore, the hypothesis that those who commit animal cruelty as children or early adolescents progress to commit violence against humans was unable to be tested in this study.

In light of these methodological and theoretical shortcomings and issues, how should we think about the link? In my view, the best evidence to date suggests that the majority of those who abuse animals, at least in their youth, do so infrequently, outgrow it, and typically go on to lead "normal" lives. And if we adopt an overly psychopathological explanation of animal cruelty, we are likely to focus on the most extreme forms of violence and the most troubled perpetrators, at the risk of ignoring the more common forms and causes of abuse.

Yet animal abuse and interpersonal violence do often go together. Animal abuse can be a risk factor, a marker, and sometimes a precursor of other forms of violence, and vice versa. We must also remember that risk factors are not always determinative; neither are they to be disregarded (e.g., smoking is a risk factor for lung cancer). And what if a specific time order cannot be established? Nevertheless, it is still important for judges, juries, prosecutors, clinicians, child protective workers, shelter workers, veterinarians, police, and legislators to take animal abuse seriously, a point also forcefully made by Arluke and his colleagues:

Our findings should not dishearten those who wish to rally society's interests in animal abuse. On the contrary, there is much to rally around. People who commit a single known act of animal abuse—oftentimes far less torturous and sadistic than the individuals examined in classic studies in the literature, such as those by Kellert and Felthous—are more likely to commit other criminal offenses than matched participants who do not abuse animals. As a flag of potential antisocial behavior—including but not limited to violence—isolated acts of cruelty toward animals must not be ignored by judges, psychiatrists, social workers, veterinarians, police, and others who encounter cases of abuse in their work. Moreover, a link might exist between animal abuse and violence, but future research needs to tease out how often and why a subset of animal abusers subsequently commit adult violent behavior (Arluke et al., 1999, p. 973).

ISSUES AND CHALLENGES FOR
FUTURE RESEARCH ON THE LINK

Improved Conceptual and Methodological Approaches

Weak or inconsistent evidence regarding the link in part may reflect the early stage of research on animal abuse in general. A thorough discussion of those issues appears in chapter 6 (see also Ascione and Shapiro, 2009), but there is a definite need for: (a) a sound conceptual definition of animal abuse that can serve as the basis for the construction of valid and reliable measures; (b) studies that use nonclinical samples from the general population; and (c) longitudinal designs.

Beyond these more fundamental requirements, two other important and related issues are addressed below which include both methodological and ethical concerns. Methodologically, researchers must establish more specifically when and how early animal abuse may lead to subsequent violence against humans. That way, the number of false positives—those who may commit childhood animal cruelty rarely or less severely and never go on to perpetrate further violence against humans or animals—can hopefully be significantly reduced. And ethically, how do our concerns about false positives lead us to respond to children who have been identified as perpetrators of cruelty to animals?

More Specific Pathways and Abuser Characteristics

The time has come to move beyond investigating the simple association between childhood animal cruelty and subsequent human violence to research that considers other factors that may identify which forms of animal abuse and which types of abusers are likely to graduate to violence against humans. Some possibilities suggested by Merz-Perez and Heide include the "type of cruelty committed, the type of animal targeted, the motivation for the cruelty, and the perpetrator's response to the cruelty" (2004, p. 154). Recent scholarship is starting to posit and investigate more specific pathways and relationships between early animal abuse and subsequent human violence, and thus to identify more specific subsets of offending individuals (Ascione and Shapiro, 2009). For example, studies by Hensley, Tallichet, and colleagues (Hensley and Tallichet, 2009; Hensley, Tallichet, and Dutkiewicz, 2009; Tallichet and Hensley, 2004; Tallichet, Hensley, and Singer, 2005) have examined such predictors as the methods of childhood animal cruelty and recurrent violence against both animals and humans, albeit among incarcerated violent criminals.

Recurrent Acts of Violence

One study (Tallichet and Hensley, 2004) of 261 prisoners from one maximum- and two medium-security prisons sought to determine whether repeated acts of harming animals in childhood were later related to repeated acts of interpersonal violence. Recurrent interpersonal violence was operationalized as the number of times a convict had been convicted of murder or attempted murder, rape or attempted rape, and aggravated assault. Childhood or adolescent animal cruelty was measured by asking how many times the inmate had ever hurt or killed animals, other than for hunting. All of these acts occurred prior to incarceration.

In addition to how many times the inmate had committed childhood animal cruelty, other predictors of repeated interpersonal violence—race, education, urban/rural residence, parents' marital status, number of siblings, and whether the prisoner had been sent to juvenile detention—were also tested. Only two significant predictors emerged. The most important was childhood animal cruelty: the greater the number of acts of animal abuse, the greater the number of acts of interpersonal violence committed. Interestingly, the only other significant predictor was number of siblings: the greater the number of siblings, the more likely were repeated acts of interpersonal violence to be committed.

In a replication of the 2004 study, Hensley, Tallichet, and Dutkiewicz (2009) surveyed 180 inmates from one medium- and one maximum-security prison in March 2007. Recurrent interpersonal violence was operationalized slightly differently than in the 2004 study. Rather than asking the number of times inmates had been convicted of murder or attempted murder, rape or attempted rape, or assault, the survey asked the number of times they had committed each of these acts. Robbery was also added to the list of violent crimes. Demographic factors—race, education, and urban/rural residence—were included in the analysis. As in the prior study, repeated acts of animal abuse were significantly related to later repeated acts of interpersonal violence as an adult. No other variable was significant.

Forms of Animal Abuse

Hensley and Tallichet (2009) also explored whether the method of childhood animal abuse was related to repeated acts of adult interpersonal violence. Using the sample from the 2004 study above, they examined the relationship between six methods of animal cruelty—drowning, hitting or kicking, shooting, choking, burning, and having sex with an animal—and the number of times inmates had been convicted of violent crimes (defined as in the 2004 study above). Other predictors in the model included the number of times respondents had hurt or killed animals, the age when they first hurt or killed animals, and their current age. Only two variables emerged as significant predictors of multiple convictions of violent crimes as an adult. Inmates who had drowned animals or who had sex with animals as children or teens were more likely to have committed repeated acts of interpersonal violence. According to Hensley and Tallichet (2009, p. 156):

> Drowning and having sex with an animal require very similar violent means toward another species that may lead to later aggression toward humans; both are acts that involve overpowering an animal. Aggression leading to the death or near death of an animal or sexual climax by the perpetrator suggests that the animal abuser may also have been seeking some particular release from the experience. Perhaps the same release was experienced later following their aggression toward humans in adulthood.

False Positives and Labeling Children

Critics of "link" research rightly point out that not all children who abuse animals go on to live violent criminal lives. In fact, as noted earlier, most children tend to have limited experiences that they often outgrow and may even regret (Arluke, 2002). So it is the large number of what some have called "false positives"—those who abuse animals and never progress to violence toward humans—that needs to be reduced. Beyond that, however, some observers worry that early labeling of children who harm animals, based on concerns about them moving on to violence against humans, will lead to stigmatizing those children, thereby creating rather than reducing deviance (Patterson-Kane and Piper, 2009).

The types of research summarized above are attempts to further clarify the connection between childhood animal cruelty and subsequent adult violence, and thereby decreasing the number of false positives. In a similar vein, Levin and Arluke (2009) present evidence for how that might be done in the most extreme cases of the link—serial killers. From Levin and Arluke's perspective, the simplistic notion that many serial killers abused animals as children is insufficient; many did not, and many other individuals who did inflict cruelty on animals as children never became serial murderers. Levin and Arluke argue that the common denominator for serial killers who abused animals is the desire to inflict pain and suffering for pleasure. Thus, for these individuals, the violence in both cases—animals and humans—is about the sadistic exercise of power and control over others.

Consequently, it is not just harming animals but torturing them; it is not just inflicting suffering, but doing so literally in a hands-on manner; and it is not just victimizing any animal, but those, like cats and dogs, who are the most anthropomorphized in our culture. In these cases, Levin and Arluke argue, the methods of violence employed are often similar for both human and animal victims. So again, rather than focusing just on general childhood animal cruelty, Levin and Arluke call for attention to those who target cats and dogs and torture them "up close and personal," using their hands. These findings fit with the conclusions of Hensley and Tallichet presented above, suggesting the role of power and control in these violent acts.

But how does the concern about false positives mean we

should respond to children who are detected abusing animals? Patterson-Kane and Piper (2009) are concerned about the unintended negative consequences that could result if what they consider as distortions of link research are used to label and thus stigmatize children who abuse animals. Such an approach, in their view, "inevitably leads to explanations that emphasize individual pathology" (2009, p. 605).

However valid these concerns are about labeling and stigmatizing youth who inflict suffering upon animals, we must be careful not to go too far here. Patterson-Kane and Piper also make unfounded claims about how the link is already being used to scare and threaten families. They present no evidence for their assertion that "suspicion of animal abuse is beginning to constitute grounds for the removal of children, and/or for placing suspects on various child protection registers" (p. 592). The key is not *whether* to respond to children who abuse animals, but *how*.

Certainly animal abuse is an act we want to identify, discourage, and eliminate among all members of society, especially children. I tend to agree with Levin and Arluke, who insist that the false positive issue is only a problem if it

serves as a basis for stigmatizing and punishing children. If instead we reach out to youngsters who abuse animals to help them in order to give them an improved sense of self-esteem and confidence, the false positive issue is minimized. At worst, we might give a few children our assistance when it is not needed. In the process, we will also be reducing animal cruelty (2009, p. 169).

Questions for Discussion

1. Do you think that harming animals as a child or teenager makes it more likely that one will harm people later in life? Why or why not?

2. Do you think researchers have been too concerned about the alleged link between animal abuse and human violence?

3. What is the best way to deal with children who have been caught abusing animals?

5

Explaining Animal Abuse:
Theoretical Perspectives

FEMINIST THEORIES

Feminist perspectives, which have been extremely valuable in explaining domestic violence (e.g., Yllo, 1993), and violence toward women in general, have also contributed greatly to our understanding of animal abuse. From a feminist perspective the abuse of animals is part of a larger dominance and exploitation by males of less powerful others—women, children, and animals. Patriarchy has led dominant males to use violence as a means to control other less powerful individuals, including other animals. "A hierarchy in which men have power over women and humans have power over animals, is actually more appropriately understood as a hierarchy in which men have power over women, (feminized) men and (feminized) animals" (Adams, 1995, p. 80).

According to Adams (1994), hostility to the body—"somatophobia" (see Spelman, 1982)—is symptomatic of sexism, racism, classism, as well as speciesism. That hostility to "despised and disenfranchised bodies, that is, those of animals, children, women, and nondominant men" is interconnected (Adams, 1994, p. 64). She goes on to say that, "Clearly, women's oppression is interwoven with that of animals, so that women and animals are both trapped by the control exercised over their own *and* each other's bodies" (1994, p. 70, emphasis in the original).

Increasingly, empirical studies on pet abuse and woman-battering have revealed the central role of gender, power, and control in male violence toward both women and animals (Ascione, 1998; Ascione et al., 2007; Faver and Strand, 2003, 2007; Flynn, 2000a, 2000c; Loring and Bolden-Hines, 2004; Simmons and Lehmann, 2007). A man's harming of animals as a part of battering exposes the intentionality of his efforts to control his partner. Adams (1995) has identified nine ways or strategies that men control women through pet abuse. By harming animals, batterers

- demonstrate their power
- teach submission
- isolate women from supportive networks and relationships
- express their rage at women's independence
- perpetuate a climate of terror
- intimidate women to keep them from leaving
- punish women for leaving
- coerce them into observing or participating in the animals' abuse, and
- confirm their power

Batterers who also abuse pets may differ in other ways from those who do not. One study found that batterers who abused pets were more dangerous and used more controlling behaviors than men who had not (Simmons and Lehmann, 2007). Batterers who had committed pet abuse had higher rates of sexual violence, marital rape, emotional violence, and stalking. In addition, pet-abusing batterers used more controlling behaviors (e.g., male privilege, isolation, blaming, intimidation, threats, economic abuse, etc.). For men who had killed a pet, this difference was even greater.

Batterers may even coerce women to commit illegal acts by threatening their companion animals. Loring and Bolden-Hines (2004) studied 107 women who had been referred to a family violence center in Georgia specializing in legal issues in part because they had committed at least one illegal act. Of the 107, 62 percent had either currently owned pets or had in the past year, and three-fourths reported either actual or threatened pet abuse. Within this group, 24 individuals reported that they were coerced by threats and actual harm to their pets to commit such crimes as bank robbery, credit-card theft or fraud, stock fraud, bank fraud, and/or drug trafficking. All of these women said that they committed their crimes to prevent their pets from being abused.

SYMBOLIC INTERACTIONISM

Another theory that has been employed in the analysis of animal abuse is symbolic interactionism (Blumer, 1969; Mead, 1934). From this perspective, through interactions with others, individuals give meaning to their experiences and actively construct reality. To interact symbolically, and to develop a sense of self, actors must be able to take on roles—to imagine how others define the situation, including how the actors themselves are perceived by others.

Symbolic-interactionist perspectives of animal abuse have

typically focused on the meaning participants give to the concept of abuse. This focus has led to two different types of research. One approach has concentrated on how adult animal abusers account for their deviant behavior, redefining it to make it more acceptable (e.g., Forsythe and Evans, 1998). A second approach has been to ask participants who are involved in various aspects of animal abuse how they perceived their actions (Arluke, 2002, 2004, 2006). For example, when asked about their violence to animals as children, late adolescents and young adults redefined their "abuse," seeing it as a normal part of growing up (e.g., Arluke, 2002). Both strands point to the importance of (a) not imposing the researcher's meaning on the behavior or interaction being studied, (b) how respondents' definitions shape their behavior, and (c) how perpetrators' social constructions of the abusive acts are central to preserving the sense of self.

A third approach, following the lead of Sanders (1993, 1999) and Alger and Alger (1997, 1999), has challenged Mead and traditional sociological thought that only humans are capable of symbolic interaction. This new perspective argues that animals are minded, social animals that have selves, can role-take, and can create shared meanings with humans (and sometimes other animals) with whom they interact.

In my small qualitative study in the late 1990s (Flynn, 2000a), many battered women reported that their companion animals were very upset during their battering, even to the point of either trying to protect them during the attack or comfort them afterward. Their pets were capable of expressing emotion and were attuned to the women's emotional states. To the women, these responses were evidence of their pets' mindedness—intentional, reciprocal, thoughtful behavior.

Neutralizing Deviance: Dog Fighting and Cockfighting

Two forms of animal cruelty that are now illegal in every state—dog fighting and cockfighting—have received attention from sociologists (Darden and Worden, 1996; Forsythe and Evans, 1998; Hawley, 1993). In 2008, Louisiana became the last state to ban cockfighting. However, at the time of these studies, cockfighting was still legal in Arizona, Missouri, and Oklahoma. These studies are significant because they focus on the participants' perceptions of their deviance. In so doing, they examine the social construction of deviance and the meanings of the actors, and reveal the efforts that individuals make to excuse or justify their deviance, in an attempt to protect their self-image.

Neutralization theory, introduced by Sykes and Matza (1957), holds that contrary to more traditional views of deviance as a rejection of prevailing norms, individuals who violate the law really accept the conventional moral order. However, they attempt to counter the stigma of their deviance by making exceptions or rationalizations called *neutralization techniques*. According to Sykes and Matza, individuals use five techniques of neutralization to rationalize their deviant behavior. These are (a) denial of the victim (the harm was deserved, so, in reality, there is no victim), (b) denial of responsibility (the harm done was caused by an accident, mistake, or forces that were beyond the offender's control), (c) denial of injury (no one was really harmed, and thus, again, there is no real victim), (d) appeal to higher loyalties (attachment to smaller or more intimate groups takes precedence over attachment to society), and (e) condemnation of the condemners (those who denounce our behavior have engaged in acts that are equally bad or worse).

Dog Fighting

Forsythe and Evans (1998) applied neutralization theory to explore the rationalizations used by "dogmen"—men who breed and fight pit bulls. This field research, involving interviews with dogmen and observations of dog fights, took place in Louisiana—considered by many to be the center of dog fighting in the United States—as well as in Mississippi.

According to Forsythe and Evans, dogfighters utilized three techniques of neutralization—denial of injury, appeal to higher loyalties, and condemnation of the condemners. They also uncovered a fourth rationalization, which they labeled "we are good people." According to the authors, this technique "defends dogmen as good people and maintains their dog fighting is expunged by their good characters and/ or good deeds" (Forsythe and Evans, 1998, pp. 206–207).

Cockfighting

Studies of cockfighting also illustrate similar examples of neutralization. Hawley (1993) spent fifteen years doing ethnographic research on the culture of cockfighting in the southern and midwestern regions of the United States (including areas where cockfighting was still legal), as well as parts of Latin America and around the Caribbean. Darden and Worden (1996) examined cockfighting in a setting on the Oklahoma–Arkansas border. Both studies revealed that cockfighters, overwhelmingly male and rural, rationalized their criminal activity in a variety of ways, fitting with the main techniques identified by Forsythe and Evans (1998). They also raised pseudo-scientific arguments, stating that it was part of the bird's nature to fight, and that, because of the bird's simple central-nervous system, no pain was experienced (denial of injury).

Another justification was that there was a strong historical precedent in favor of cockfighting, with individuals often affirming their own status by mentioning the names of famous men who were also cockfighters—for example, George Washington, Abraham Lincoln, Andrew Jackson, Henry VIII, and Robert E. Lee (appeal to higher loyalties). Other attempts at neutralization suggested that opponents had a bias against a rural lifestyle, that government was overextending its reach into the private lives of citizens and had no right to regulate this activity (condemnation of the condemners). Cockfighters justified their deviance by claiming that animals exist for human use, often citing biblically based arguments, and that cockfighting builds character ("we are good people"). Thus, like dogfighters, cockfighters attempt to minimize their deviance by redefining it, thereby maintaining their positive self-images.

Definitions of the Participants
Animal Abuse as Normative
Although most research on animal abuse proceeds from the assumption that such behavior is pathological and deviant, Arluke (2002) presents an alternative view. Drawing on a symbolic interactionist perspective, which argues that a full

understanding of human behavior depends on knowing how the participants define their actions, Arluke suggests that it is also possible to frame animal abuse by children and adolescents as normative and instrumental. As Arluke states, "[L]umping together all instances of harming animals as impulsive and pathological does not allow for the possibility that abuse can be instrumental and normative, in the sense that abusers may gain things from their acts that the larger society supports and defines as essential" (p. 406).

To determine what young people gain from animal abuse, Arluke interviewed 25 college undergraduates who were screened from two large introductory sociology classes at a large, urban northeastern university, about their past abuse of animals. The participants were predominately white, male, and middle class. In analyzing these interviews, Arluke concluded that animal abuse is a form of "dirty play" (see Fine, 1986), through which children attempt to appropriate adult identities and culture. By asserting their autonomy and control over not only their own lives, but also animals' lives, adolescents were enabled through harming animals to resist and challenge adult authority and the standards of the adult world.

Through their abuse of animals, youths appropriate four kinds of adultlike powers: "keeping adultlike secrets, drawing adultlike boundaries, doing adultlike activities, and gathering and confirming adultlike knowledge" (Arluke, 2002, p. 413).

- *Keeping adultlike secrets*—Animals were abused to experience the thrill of not getting caught, not as an end in itself, and this was empowering. The youths' shared secret of "getting away with" abuse allowed respondents to exercise their independence from, while at the same time incorporating essential aspects of, the adult culture.

- *Drawing adultlike boundaries*—Through their abuse, children learn the significance of classifying others as "not us," which justifies differential and sometimes exploitative treatment. Many respondents abused animals with peers and playmates, indicating that the companionship and peer approval was more important to them than the actual abuse. So animal abuse enabled children to draw boundaries that marked not only who was excluded, but also who was included as part of the in-group.

- *Doing adultlike activities*—Many respondents likened their animal abuse to such adult behaviors as hunting or physically disciplining children that had overstepped their boundaries. Others saw their abuse as a way to develop skills that would be required for success in the adult world of work, such as emotional detachment. As with the other types of appropriation, once again animal abuse was not an end in itself, but as a means to rehearse their future adult statuses.

- *Gathering and confirming adultlike knowledge*— Animal abuse was a way for individuals to gather and confirm information from adults, making sure adults had not only been truthful with them, but had not kept things from them. Respondents often talked about their abuse as a form of experimentation, illustrating once again that their cruelty to animals was undertaken to acquire adultlike knowledge through adultlike methods.

Interestingly, Arluke's respondents displayed two different responses to their past abusive behaviors. Some individuals felt bad about their behavior, with some remembering their guilt at the time, while others reported feeling guilty now because they didn't remember feeling guilty at the time they committed the abuse. By redefining their "dirty play" as behavior that is offensive rather than fun, some participants were able to present themselves as mature, moral young adults. Others, however, still referred to their abuse of animals as fun and exhibited little evidence of remorse, seeing their animal abuse as a normal part of childhood that they had simply outgrown, and for which they had absolved themselves. These two different forms of self-presentation reflect not maturational differences in the respondents, Arluke argues, but rather the ambivalent and paradoxical attitudes about animals that exist in American society.

Other Participants

In his later work, Arluke (2004, 2006) continued to challenge conventional approaches to cruelty that employ objective, psychological models that view animal abuse as a clearly definable act committed by crazy or troubled individuals. Instead, he insightfully uncovers and reveals the subjective meanings of cruelty from the various perspectives of individuals who are participants in some part of the process. Expanding on his work with college students, Arluke (2006) explored the meaning of cruelty among humane law enforcement agents (animal control officers), hoarders, shelter workers, and humane-society marketers. In this way, Arluke helps us to understand not just how animal cruelty can have different meanings for different people at different times and in different circumstances, but how these definitions help to shape the identities of the participants and reveal the inconsistent attitudes toward humans and other animals in the larger society.

- *Animal Control Officers*, dubbed "animal cops" by Arluke, begin their careers believing they are legitimate authority figures who can make a difference in the lives of animals. However, they are soon overwhelmed and disillusioned by trivial complaints that don't measure up to their definitions of "real" or "legal" cruelty, combined with a public who doesn't understand the agents' role, perceiving them either as "wannabe cops" or "animal extremists." Initially, as a result of these competing meanings, agents try to minimize their authority to offer advice and instruction, more like humane educators. Eventually, however, this approach proves ineffective, and most agents take advantage of the ambiguity of their role and "bluff power"—that is, asserting more authority than they know they legally have—in order to bring about more favorable outcomes for animals.

- *Hoarders* are viewed by the public as bad, mad, or sad because they collect and neglect large numbers of animals. Yet the hoarders reframe their cruelty as "kindness and sacrifice" and actively reconstruct their identities as "saints," thereby attempting to redefine their public image by justifying and excusing their behaviors.

- *Shelter workers* from two types of shelters—no-kill versus open-admission—revealed the different meanings operating in each. No-kill workers see euthanizing healthy animals that could be adopted into loving homes as cruel and thus the identities of those who do euthanize are tainted. Open-admission shelter workers, on the other hand, see no-kill shelters much like private schools that can select only the "best" prospects for adoption; or as warehouses, where the animal's extensive time in a cage is interpreted as crueler than ending suffering through euthanasia. Because of the challenges of their work and these contested meanings, both groups must struggle with how to manage their emotions and preserve their sense of themselves as "good people."

- *Marketers* for humane societies strive to find the "beautiful" case—the one with all the right elements for evoking a supportive emotional and financial response from the public. These cases, where appealing animals who have experienced horrendous abuse survive to be adopted into good homes thanks to the heroic efforts of agents, shelter workers, and others, can serve to validate identities, strengthen morale, and create solidarity in the humane community.

Arluke's research demonstrates that understanding cruelty against animals, or any social phenomenon, depends on understanding the events from the viewpoint of those involved. Traditional, psychological approaches that see animal abuse committed by "sick" individuals do not tell the whole story about these horrible acts against nonhuman animals. As we have seen, most childhood animal abusers, for example, do not grow up to be serial killers or wife abusers or even juvenile delinquents. Rejecting the notion that there is a standard, objective definition of animal cruelty, Arluke identifies competing meanings and their consequences for individuals (both human and nonhuman) and institutions. Multiple definitions of cruelty can (a) create conflict, for example, between animal control officers and the public, hoarders and more "normal" pet owners, and no-kill and open-admission shelter workers; (b) be resources for identity construction; and (c) illustrate the contradictory attitudes we hold as a society about our relationships with other animals.

COMBINING THE TWO APPROACHES: A FEMINIST-INTERACTIONIST EXPLANATION OF WOMAN-BATTERING AND PET ABUSE

Traditionally, research on animal abuse has conceptualized animals as tools of violence, whose abuse is evidence of psychiatric illness, and has been seen as important only because of its connection with humans, rather than seeing other animals as individuals whose lives and victimization are worthy of scholarly attention and moral consideration in their own right, and who are legitimate partners in relationships with battered women. This perspective is harmful to the women as well as the animals, as it tends to devalue their nonhuman relationships, which may be the most meaningful and valuable ones in their lives.

The goal is to bring the companion animals of battered women to the center of the analysis by examining the connections between women's and animals' victimization and by seeing nonhuman animals as individuals (as "persons") and as relationship partners. Clearly, feminist-theoretical perspectives have been invaluable in helping to explain interpersonal violence, including woman-battering and pet abuse. As noted above, studies on pet abuse and woman-battering have revealed the powerful roles of gender, power, and control in explaining male violence toward both women and animals. Yet the argument here is that the picture would be more complete if it included a view of animals that sees them as competent, legitimate partners in intimate relationships with humans—that is, a combination of feminist theory and symbolic interactionism (see Brennan, 2007).

Animals as Individuals and Relationship Partners

Because symbolic interaction, according to Mead, requires the ability to speak, sociologists in general and interactionists in particular have limited their study of close relationships to those existing only between humans. Yet Clinton Sanders (2003) has taken issue with this view, arguing that it excludes an extremely common and important type of close relationship—the one between humans and other animals. This relationship has, Sanders contends, all of the central qualities that characterize other human close relationships: namely, interactions that are frequent, diverse, intense (emotional), and which endure over time (Kelley et al., 1983). According to Sanders (2003):

> I maintain that this characterization of close relationships [existing only between human beings] is overly restrictive. It excludes from consideration a class of affiliations that are commonplace, imbued with emotion, and central to the shaping of the identities and selves of those involved. Traditionally, conventional sociologists have ignored or denigrated relationships between people and their companion animals. However, the intense, involving, and routine interactions forming these relations are worthy of serious attention and have the potential of adding significantly to the sociology of intimate exchanges (p. 406).

Why are humans and companion animals able to establish routine and patterned interactions? That is, how are they able to form close relationships? Increasingly, sociologists such as Sanders (1993, 1999, 2003), Alger and Alger (1997, 1999), and Irvine (2004) have challenged Mead and traditional sociological thought, arguing that animals are minded, social actors who have selves, can role-take, can create shared meanings with humans (and sometimes other animals) with whom they interact, and thus are also capable of interacting symbolically.

In their work with caretakers of severely disabled family members, Bogdan and Taylor (1989) argued that caretakers, in the absence of spoken language, construct a social identity that enables them to see the disabled as minded and as still capable of engaging in interaction. According to Bogdan and Taylor, the four features of this process of attributing "personhood" to nonverbal, disabled others involve seeing them as: (a) minded, social actors; (b) individuals with unique personalities; (c) reciprocating partners in the relationship; and (d) legitimate relationship partners who are afforded a social place in the family.

Both Sanders (1993), in his study of dog caretakers, and the Algers (Alger and Alger, 1997), in their study of feline caretakers, found that both groups attributed personhood to their companion animals. Both dog and cat owners considered their animals to be thinking individuals who contributed to the relationship, and who were seen as members of the family.

Studies of battered women with pets offer evidence that these women similarly regard their companion animals as "people." Most women think of their pets as family members, as their children. In my earlier qualitative study (Flynn, 2000a), two respondents even brought photo albums to the interview that were filled with pictures of their companion animals—much like a parent memorializing the experiences of their human child. They described their animals as intelligent individuals with their own personalities. Many battered women saw their companion animals as being very upset upon witnessing the woman's battering, often trying to protect her during the attack or comfort her afterward. Their pets were capable of expressing emotion and were attuned to the women's emotional states. The women saw these actions as evidence of their pets' mindedness—intentional, reciprocal, thoughtful behavior.

As noted earlier, given their social isolation, battered women are likely to have limited opportunities for meaningful human interaction. Similarly, their low self-esteem may also prevent them from maintaining strong relationships with others. So their relationship with their companion animals may be particularly important and valued. One recent study found that companion animals actually helped reduce the likelihood of suicidal thinking and behavior among abused women (Fitzgerald, 2007).

When animals are threatened or harmed, it is not merely a prized possession or a sentimental object that may be lost. As Carol Adams (1995) recognized, "What is so anguishing to the human victim about the injury of an animal is that it is a threat or actual destruction of a cherished relationship in which the animal has been seen as an individual" (p. 59). Yet it is precisely because the women view their pets as people—as individuals, as valued relationship partners, as family members—that the abuse of the animal is so terrifying and so effective. Batterers, perhaps as well as anyone, understand the power of this relationship, and unfortunately are able to use it to create a climate of terror in the home. Adams notes that "The degree to which she or the children have an intense respectful relationship with an animal is the extent to which he can harm her by harming the animal" (Adams, 1995, p. 77).

But even when women escape to a shelter, the trauma does not end. Since few shelters allow women to bring their pets, they are forced to leave them behind. For many women (anywhere from 4–50 percent, depending on the study), this often means leaving their pets with the abusive partner or ex-partner. Understandably, this creates much anxiety and concern among the women, who are not only worried about their animals' well-being, but who are now also vulnerable to batterers' attempts to control them by threatening to harm their companion animals. And even if the animal is in better or more trusted care, the women (and their children) are separated from and concerned about their nonhuman companion.

All of these features—a pet with whom women share a close relationship, who is abused (and sometimes killed), who often cannot be protected and must be left behind—combine to create a powerful form of emotional abuse that includes fear, guilt, and grief (Faver and Strand, 2003). Many battered women have reported that their children had witnessed their companion animals' victimization and, like the women, the children were both angered and terrified. In many ways, the impact of children witnessing the violence toward their animal companions parallels the effects of wife abuse on children. Not only was a loved one—a valued member of the family—being harmed, but they were powerless to do anything about it at the time and were often prevented from comforting the animal immediately following the abuse. In general, the abuse contributed to a climate of control, intimidation, and terror for the children, women, and animals.

Because women and children strongly consider their companion animals to be members of the family, pet abuse should be not be conceptualized as just another type of wife or child abuse, but also as a separate form of family violence in itself. And not only does harming animals harm women, but pets were also victimized when women were abused. Witnessing a woman's abuse is often very emotionally upsetting for her animal companion. During an abusive episode, pets often react by shivering or shaking, cowering, hiding, or urinating—similar physical manifestations of stress that are displayed by humans. Therefore, it is important to understand that both women and animals are victimized by the abuse of the other. A man's violence toward an animal also hurts his partner (and children), just as his violence toward her also hurts the animal.

Implications for Theory and Research

The acknowledgment that other animals are individuals and legitimate relationship partners creates exciting and challenging opportunities for researchers. In this situation, animal abuse is no longer relevant merely as an indicator of human psychopathology or an instrument of male power and control over women, but as another form of violence against individuals who can experience terror and pain, and should receive attention for that reason alone. Scholars can begin to study animal abuse and its relation to family violence from the point of view of the animals themselves. In general, researchers need to expand their notion of personhood and to broaden their conception of close relationships, following the lead of researchers like Sanders and Leslie Irvine (2004), the latter who makes a compelling argument for companion animal "selfhood."

When companion animals are viewed as minded, social actors; as individuals with unique personalities who are reciprocating and intentional, rather than as objects or tools or commodities, then they are more likely to become full participants in close relationships with humans, and less likely to be harmed. It is also important for researchers of domestic violence to acknowledge and examine the relationship that battered women have with their companion animals.

AGNEW'S SOCIAL-PSYCHOLOGICAL THEORY OF ANIMAL ABUSE

To date, only Robert Agnew (1998) has put forward a full-fledged theory of animal abuse. Agnew's social-psychological theory draws heavily on leading criminological theories such as social-learning theory, strain theory, and control theory to help explain why individuals abuse animals. He argues that the causes of animal abuse should be examined not only because animal abuse is correlated with human interpersonal violence, but also because animals are worthy of moral consideration irrespective of their relationship to humans.

Agnew's theorizing is groundbreaking in another way—with regard to his definition of animal abuse. Departing from traditional definitions that have conceptualized abuse as being behavior that is socially unacceptable, intentional, and/or unnecessary, and which is committed by individuals or small groups, Agnew instead broadly defines animal abuse as "any act that contributes to the pain or death of an animal or that otherwise threatens the welfare of an animal" (p. 179). This definition, from Agnew's perspective, has several advantages: it includes the actions that account for the vast majority of harm inflicted against animals (factory farming, animal experimentation, etc.); it is not linked to current beliefs that would be shaped by social actors with the most power; and it does not limit abuse only to illegal behaviors.

Agnew's theory begins with three individual factors that are directly related to increasing the likelihood that an individual will harm animals. These three propositions are derived from the animal-abuse literature, as well as from social-learning theory and neutralization theory. Animal abuse is more likely to occur when individuals are (a) ignorant of the abusive consequences of their actions, or (b) believe their abusive treatment is justified, and (c) when they perceive that the benefits of their actions outweigh the costs.

A second set of factors helps to explain the variation in the abuse caused by the first set of intervening variables. These variables, whose effects are both direct and indirect, include (a) individual traits, such as empathy, impulsivity, or self-control; (b) socialization; (c) strain or stress; (d) level of social control; and (e) the nature of the animal.

Finally, Agnew incorporates structural factors related to one's social position that are associated with animal abuse— gender, age, race, education, occupation, urban/rural residence, and region. Social-position variables may directly affect the three immediate causes of animal abuse, but more often they indirectly influence these factors via their effect on the second set of factors (individual traits, socialization, etc.).

Agnew cautions that this model is a general one and that it is based on conclusions drawn from limited empirical research undertaken over a decade ago. For example, future studies might refine the categories of socially acceptable versus unacceptable animal abuse and seek to determine the factors that are more likely to be predictors of each form. For example, ignorance about the consequences of abusing animals may be more helpful in explaining socially acceptable harm, which is usually indirect. However, strain, social control, and individual characteristics may better explain socially unacceptable animal abuse, which is typically direct and intentional. Other possible hypotheses might address the relationships between variables—for example, the greater the benefits of the abuse for an individual, the more likely one may be to distance oneself from the abuse, using neutralization techniques to justify one's actions. Or perhaps harm resulting from strain "caused" by the animal is more likely when the abuse is seen as justified. Finally, future research might examine how cultural norms regarding animals support their mistreatment by asking how the structure and practices of social institutions (e.g., the government, economy, education, religion, and science) reinforce and perpetuate animal abuse.

Agnew's theory represents an impressive effort to systematically explain animal abuse. His significant work should serve to generate many additional hypotheses for future researchers, and it provides a solid theoretical foundation onto which scholars can continue to build.

Questions for Discussion

1. Gender, power, and control appear to be operating in various forms regarding the connection between animal abuse and human violence—for example, woman-battering and pet abuse, animal abuse and bullying, and childhood animal cruelty and subsequent violent criminality.

What are the dynamics that might explain the role of these variables?

2. Arluke argues that childhood animal abuse could be seen as normative. What does he mean by that? Do you agree?

3. Come up with three hypotheses based on Agnew's social-psychological theory of animal abuse.

6

Recommendations for Policy and Professionals and Directions for Future Research

POLICY RECOMMENDATIONS

Laws and Legal Professionals

Policy makers should strengthen laws and penalties for those who engage in abusive behavior toward animals. As of 2011, animal-cruelty statutes in forty-seven states (plus the District of Columbia, Puerto Rico, and the Virgin Islands) include felony-level offenses (Animal Legal Defense Fund [ALDF], 2011; Humane Society of the United States, 2011). Only Idaho, North Dakota, and South Dakota have failed to enact felony animal-abuse legislation. This is a dramatic increase since the early 1990s, when fewer than ten states had felony animal-abuse statutes. In many cases, stiffer penalties for animal cruelty have been successfully enacted, in part by relying on claims that such cruelty is a likely indicator of a tendency toward future interpersonal violence.

A ranking of all fifty states (and U.S. territories) based on the overall strength and comprehensiveness of their animal protection laws has been undertaken every year since 2006 by the Animal Legal Defense Fund (see Figure following). According to the ALDF, the best five states, in order, are Illinois, Maine, Michigan, Oregon, and California, while the five worst are South Dakota, Iowa, Idaho, North Dakota, and Kentucky.

2011 U.S. Animal Protection Laws Rankings™
Comparing Overall Strength & Comprehensiveness

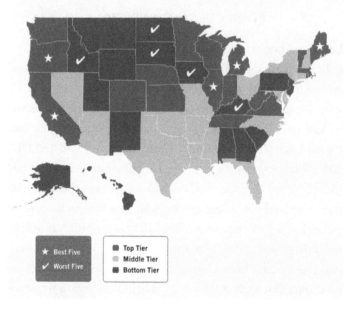

Source: 2011 State Animal Protection Laws Rankings. Copyright © 2012 Animal Legal Defense Fund.

Courts need to value companion animals and women's relationships with them as they consider issues of divorce, custody, and restraining orders. For example, the abuse of companion animals should be seen as powerful evidence of parental unfitness and could be used as a valuable tool to help battered women retain the family home and obtain orders of protection for themselves, their children, and their pets. With the limited success that battered women have traditionally experienced in the criminal-justice system, stricter enforcement of laws against male batterers' abuse of the family pet could be a powerful weapon that enables prosecutors to more successfully convict perpetrators who previously have managed to escape responsibility for their violence. Evidence of animal cruelty could improve prosecutors' chances of securing an order of protection, custody of the home and children for the victim, and the arrest of the batterer. Pets are increasingly being included in orders of protection. As of August 2011, twenty-one states, including the District of Columbia and Puerto Rico, have enacted legislation that includes provisions for pets in domestic violence protection orders (Wisch, 2011).

Recognizing the link between animal abuse and family violence should lead to the cross-training and cross-referrals between animal-control officers and human-service professionals. Policies that enable the sharing of information between both groups of professionals could result in a more effective response to human and animal victims of violence. According to the National Link Coalition (Arkow, 2011), as of August 2011, three states mandated cross-reporting—West Virginia, Illinois, and Connecticut. Several other states require that child-protection professionals report animal abuse (Louisiana, Massachusetts, Nebraska, and Tennessee), while others require animal-control officials to report child abuse (California, Colorado, Ohio, and Virginia). In still other states (Maine, California, and Oregon), child-protection professionals *may* report animal abuse, and in Maine, animal-control officials *may* report child abuse, but in neither case is it mandatory. (See Zilney and Zilney, 2005 for a study of cross-reporting in Canada.)

Courts are increasingly ordering convicted animal abusers to receive counseling as part of their sentence. As of 2011, twenty-seven states either mandate or recommend that judges order counseling for individuals who have been convicted of animal cruelty.

With regard to legal policy, the law, judges, and prosecutors must recognize animals as legitimate victims of criminal behavior. Yet this requires more than just taking animal abuse more seriously, which undoubtedly needs to be done. The status of animals in the law must be elevated. As long as companion animals are recognized as property and not "persons," as furniture rather than family, their abuse will likely continue with minimal consequences.

Animal abuse should be taken seriously not just because of our concern for humans. Lax enforcement of animal-cruelty laws leads to untold suffering by nonhuman animals, and those who perpetrate such horrible acts should be punished, irrespective of their link to other forms of violence against humans.

Clinicians and Human-Service Professionals

Questions about animals and animal abuse should be included in assessment interviews in all social-work settings—child-protective services, adult-protective services, schools, mental health clinics, medical clinics and hospitals, domestic-violence shelters and hotlines, and juvenile-justice centers (Faver and Strand, 2008). One study of battered-women's shelters found that while the shelter-staff members may be aware of the link between animal abuse and domestic violence, few asked about pet abuse at intake or offered services for their clients with pets (Ascione, Weber, and Wood, 1997).

Further, those who work with clients with pets need to take women's (and their children's) relationships with their companion animals seriously. Shelter workers, for example, should not only ask women whether they have pets, but also respect those relationships. Women who have left their batterer to come to a shelter, particularly those without children and whose pets have been abused, do not need the added burden of having their emotional responses (worry, guilt, fear, concern, or even grief) over their companion animals dismissed or taken lightly. Understanding the importance of battered women's relationships with their pets, particularly since a significant minority delay leaving out of concern for their animals, should lead all shelters to provide services for companion animals. Although few battered-women's shelters allow on-site housing of pets, increasing numbers are establishing foster programs for their clients' pets (Ascione et al., 2007; Kogan, McConnell, Schoenfeld-Tacher, and Jansen-Lock, 2004).

In discussing the implications of battered women's close relationships with their pets for social workers, Strand and Faver (2005) stress the importance of assessing the level of attachment that women, and even their children, have with a pet. Higher levels of attachment may affect women's decisions to come to the shelter and their emotional response to being separated from their companion animals. According to Strand and Faver (2005, p. 54):

If battered women indicate that (a) their pets are like children, (b) their pets are family members, (c) their pets got them through a difficult time or a major life transition in the past, (d) they "rescued" or "were rescued" by their pet, or (e) they had a significantly difficult time grieving at the loss of a former pet, then it is likely that these women have a strong attachment to their pets.

Shelters also should expand their services to include the practical needs of pet owners. The majority of shelters do not provide temporary or emergency shelter or emergency services for the pets of clients. Given that pets of shelter clients are likely to have received lower levels of veterinary care (Ascione, Weber, and Wood, 1997) and that many pets may still be at risk for harm since they continue to reside with the batterer, the lack of such services could be doubly harmful. Shelters should establish collaborative arrangements with local animal shelters or foster-care volunteers to provide temporary housing for pets, and with local veterinarians to provide medical care.

Clinicians who work with children, and particularly counselors and social-service providers who work directly with victims of child abuse or wife abuse need to ask questions about the presence of violence against animals. Counseling programs should help battered women deal with the range of emotions that are likely to accompany the loss of, or separation from, a pet. Children of battered women may need attention, either because they could be traumatized by witnessing animal abuse or because they may have learned to inflict it themselves (Ascione, 1998; Ascione, Weber, and Wood, 1997).

Counselors should be aware that children who are cruel to animals may have the propensity for other types of interpersonal violence. Both perpetrating and witnessing animal cruelty can have potentially harmful psychological consequences that could linger for some time. Possible reactions to experiencing animal abuse include a sense of loss, guilt over not being able to prevent the abuse, grief, or even the absence of any emotional response.

Counseling programs for perpetrators, especially juveniles, are also important. The first and most successful professional psychological intervention and most successful program for adult animal abusers—the *AniCare Model of Treatment for Animal Abuse*—was developed in 1999 (Jory and Randour, 1999). Shortly thereafter, *AniCare Child* was developed for juvenile offenders under the age of seventeen (Randour, Krinsk, and Wolf, 2002). Similar to approaches used with spouse batterers, the *AniCare* program employs a cognitive-behavioral approach using direct interventions that focus on the client's need to accept accountability for his or her behavior. *AniCare*, which involves both assessment and treatment, addresses seven major concepts: accountability, respect/freedom, reciprocity, accommodation, empathy, attachment, and nurturance.

Educators

It is essential that educators are aware of, and take seriously, animal abuse and its connection with violence and other problems facing children and families. As noted previously, over 60 percent of American households contain companion animals, and the vast majority of animals are viewed as members of the family. Families with school-age children and adolescents are particularly likely to have pets, so there is a clear potential for abusive interactions involving animals and family members. Beyond that, school personnel should keep in mind the link between harming animals and bullying, remembering that animal abuse is connected both to *being a bully* and *being bullied*.

Reducing and preventing interpersonal violence may depend in part on our ability to teach and reinforce respectful and compassionate treatment of all living beings, human and animal. If cruelty to animals is related to interpersonal aggression, then perhaps the inverse is true as well. That is, encouraging positive, empathic interactions with animals in childhood may serve to reduce related or subsequent violence committed against both human and animals. In one yearlong humane-education program, for certain elementary grades, children not only demonstrated more positive attitudes toward animals, but this change also was related to greater human-directed empathy (Ascione, 1992). As Beirne has suggested, "Indeed, a plausible corollary of the progression thesis . . . is that children who have, or who are taught to have, compassion for animals might be more likely to become adults who act more sensitively and more gently toward humans" (Beirne, 2004, p. 55).

Increasingly, colleges and universities are offering courses and programs in Human–Animal Studies that focus on animal abuse and its connection to human violence at both the graduate and undergraduate level (see the website for the Animals and Society Institute for a full listing—www.animalsandsociety.org/haslinks). For example, the School of Social

Work at Arizona State University has a Graduate Certificate program in Treating Animal Abuse where advanced human-service professionals are trained to work with children and adults who have abused animals.

Similarly, the University of Denver Graduate School of Social Work offers an Animal-Assisted Social Work Certificate as part of its Master's in Social Work program. It includes coverage of the link between animal abuse and violence toward people. The Institute for Human–Animal Connection is a center devoted to research and training regarding various aspects of the human–animal interaction, including animal abuse and its relationship to other forms of violence.

Finally, the Institute for Humane Education (IHE), founded by Zoe Weil, has been training humane educators since 1996. IHE created the first humane-education training certificate program in the U.S., in addition to offering the first Master of Education in Humane Education. Offered in conjunction with Valparaiso University, the five degree-and-certificate programs are the only graduate programs in humane education in the United States and Canada (see the website for IHE, http://humaneeducation.org/sections/view/graduateprograms).

DIRECTIONS FOR FUTURE RESEARCH

The possible topics awaiting empirical investigation are limitless. For starters, we need to learn more about the structural causes of animal abuse. For example, very little is known about the role of race and ethnicity in explaining animal cruelty. Similarly, knowledge about cultural and subcultural norms could aid in the understanding of differences in the incidence of and response to animal abuse between different societies or between social groups within societies. In addition, what is the role of the media in influencing the public's knowledge of and reaction to animal cruelty?

More practical research possibilities might analyze the effectiveness of anti-cruelty laws and other social policies that deal with animal abuse. Has the increase in felony-level animal-cruelty offenses resulted in increased prosecution and conviction rates? Have laws mandating the cross-reporting of animal abuse by human-service professionals led to increased detection of animal abuse? Has mandatory counseling for juvenile offenders been effective?

Defining Animal Abuse

Much like the early years of family-violence research, studies on animal abuse have been plagued by definitional problems. As noted earlier (Agnew, 1998), conceptualizations of animal cruelty or abuse have generally incorporated three dimensions: whether the action was intentional, whether it was necessary, and whether it was socially acceptable. In the most widely used definition, Ascione (1993, p. 28) defines animal cruelty as "socially unacceptable behavior that intentionally causes unnecessary pain, suffering, or distress to and/ or death of an animal." Under this definition, neglect would be included, but only if it were intentional. Yet this definition excludes the legal, socially acceptable behaviors (which are often deemed "necessary") that cause the most harm to animals—for example, factory farming, hunting, or animal experimentation.

Vermeulen and Odendaal (1993) proposed the following definition of companion-animal abuse: the "intentional, malicious, or irresponsible, as well as unintentional or ignorant, infliction of physiological and/or psychological pain, suffering, deprivation, and the death of a companion animal by humans." While this broader definition encompasses behaviors regardless of the intent of the abuser, or of the perceived necessity or acceptability of the action by the abuser and society, it is limited to companion animals.

Researchers need to refine their conceptual definitions, addressing some of the following issues:

- What specific behaviors are included as abusive?
- Should psychological and emotional abuse be incorporated alongside physical violence?
- Should abuse be restricted only to behaviors that are intentional?
- Is animal abuse confined only to certain species? Only companion animals? Only vertebrates?
- Is abuse limited to actions committed only by individuals or small groups, or should systemic acts of institutional-level violence be included?
- Should definitions of abuse be restricted by current social norms, or should any harm to animals, regardless of its social acceptability, perceived necessity, or legal status be considered?

As noted earlier, the definition offered by Agnew discussed earlier—"any act that contributes to the pain or death of an animal or that otherwise threatens the welfare of an animal"—

avoids the problems of previous definitions. Adopting a broader and more inclusive definition of animal abuse has the advantages of including actions that are socially acceptable, legal, and account for the most harm, both at the individual and institutional level. This would encompass actions like hunting, as well as factory farming and animal experimentation. Further, definitions of animal abuse would not be linked to current beliefs that are shaped by humans with the most power.

Measurement and Samples

As a result of this definitional confusion, operational definitions of animal abuse have also been problematic. Research that relies on official records of criminal animal cruelty to operationalize abuse limits abuse only to illegal behavior, and as we know from the domestic-violence literature, there is much maltreatment that is not criminal. In addition, there is considerable variability in the anti-cruelty statutes from state to state. Most importantly, official records tend to both distort and underestimate the actual incidence and nature of animal cruelty, as only the most horrific and visible cases are included, while multiple incidents and less extreme cases often go undetected (Beirne, 2004).

There is a need for valid and reliable measures of animal abuse. Most studies relying on self-reports from individuals have employed a variety of different instruments, while other studies, particularly those early on, operationalized abuse using only a single item. Standardized measures are needed not only to have reliable data on the incidence and prevalence of animal abuse, but also for meaningful comparisons to be made across studies and populations.

A few such measures have been developed in the past decade or so. One is P.E.T. (Physical and Emotional Tormenting against animals) Scale (Baldry, 2004), developed for use with Italian schoolchildren. It is a nine-item scale, five of which measure direct animal abuse (harming, tormenting, bothering, hitting, and being cruel to animals), while four measure witnessing animal abuse (by father, mother, peers, or other adults). Respondents use a five-point Likert-type scale ranging from 1 (never) to 5 (very often) to indicate how often they have engaged in or witnessed others engage in the specified behaviors. According to Baldry, "[T]he scale was developed to have an easy-to-administer instrument intended not for clinical diagnosis but for the measurement of the prevalence and frequency of different types of abuse—including the more subtle and less-researched types of abuse such as tormenting or bothering an animal by adolescents aged 11 to 18 years" (2004, p. 11).

Two other assessments of note are the Cruelty to Animals Inventory (CAI; Dadds et al., 2004), which includes both parent-report and child-self-report versions and a parent-report instrument developed by Guymer, Mellor, Luk, and Pearse (2001). Both of these measures were created for research on Australian children and both were based on the Children and Animals Assessment Instrument (CAAI; Ascione et al., 1997), a semi-structured interview for children that assesses nine dimensions of cruelty as identified by Ascione and his colleagues: severity, frequency, duration, recency, diversity across and within categories, animal sentience level, covertness, isolation, and empathy.

When using self-report surveys to study animal abuse committed by children, researchers also need to be aware of who the respondent is. Lower rates of abuse are obtained when parents report on their children's violence toward animals than when children report on their own behavior, suggesting that parents may underestimate their children's cruelty (Ascione, 2001; Baldry, 2003).

There is a great need for national data, based on probability samples, comparable to research on family violence (Gelles and Straus, 1988; Straus, Gelles, and Steinmetz, 1980). The need for better conceptual and operational definitions of animal cruelty is necessarily connected to the requirement for better data and more representative samples. Although more studies are employing nonclinical samples of schoolchildren and college students, a significant number of studies are still conducted on clinical and criminal populations. As of this writing, only one study has examined the incidence of animal abuse utilizing a national, representative sample of American adults (Vaughn et al., 2009). Even this study used data collected for another purpose and employed a single item to measure animal abuse. As Beirne noted, the government has not generated any data on the occurrence of animal abuse. "Indeed, no technologically advanced society has generated large-scale, police-based data on the incidence and prevalence of animal abuse. There are no large-scale self-report studies on animal abuse, no household victimization surveys" (Beirne, 2004, p. 41). Finally, virtually all of the studies attempting to establish a connection between animal abuse and other types of violence, either as a cause or effect, have been retrospective or cross-sectional in nature. No longitudinal studies have yet been conducted to address this question.

Qualitative Research

Although the issues raised above regarding measurement, sampling, and research design are concerned with quantitative research, it is equally important that qualitative methods be employed as well. As studies by Arluke and others have shown, the meanings of the participants involved in animal abuse are essential to understanding and explaining their behavior. This includes not only perpetrators, but others whose perspectives are relevant, including abusers' parents and other family members; battered women with companion animals; law-enforcement and animal-control officers, as well as prosecutors and judges. In these efforts, researchers should not forget to explore ways to include the perspective of the central victims—the animals themselves.

Theory and Theory Development

Clearly, much overlap exists between animal abuse and other types of interpersonal violence, particularly family violence. Consequently, theoretical approaches from the domestic-violence arena are likely to have promise for investigations of animal abuse. Further, decades of family-violence scholarship have shown that, like violence among intimates, animal cruelty cannot be fully explained by relying exclusively on psychological models. Theory development based on social and cultural factors will be essential.

The family-violence literature also tells us that observing interparental violence is associated not only with violent behavior (Straus, Gelles, and Steinmetz, 1980), but also with more acceptable attitudes toward violence (Owens and Straus, 1975). Early studies on witnessing animal abuse have uncovered similar effects (Baldry, 2003; Flynn, 2000b). Observing animal abuse in childhood has been linked not only to childhood animal cruelty, but also to bullying and juvenile delinquency, particularly in boys. Moreover, limited empirical evidence has revealed that students often are upset about witnessing animal abuse long after its occurrence, and are bothered more by observing someone else abuse an animal in the past than they are by their own past cruelty (Flynn, 2000b). Thus theories need to be developed that explain not only animal abuse, but also its effects on those who are exposed to it.

Beyond family-violence paradigms, there are major sociological and criminological theories that should prove fruitful when applied to animal abuse. As we have seen, symbolic interactionist and feminist perspectives have much to offer. And Agnew's (1998) theory of animal abuse provides an excellent framework for theory development, drawing on such popular criminological theories such as strain theory and social-control theory. Its proposed hypotheses offer a tremendous opportunity for refinement through empirical research. Some potential avenues for further investigation were offered in chapter 5.

Other theories from related areas may have promise in the animal-abuse arena as well. One possibility is Straus's (1991, 1994) "cultural spillover theory." According to Straus, high levels of culturally approved violence may lead to a spillover effect into illegitimate violence. For example, states with the highest level of legitimate violence—that is, noncriminal, socially approved violence, as measured by such indicators as hunting licenses sold, circulation rates for magazines with violent content, execution rates, and laws permitting corporal punishment in schools—also have higher homicide rates (Baron and Straus, 1988). Additionally, children who were spanked more frequently by their parents—another form of legitimate violence—were more likely to engage in violent acts as adolescents and adults. A similar relationship may exist with regard to animal abuse. The more we harm animals in ways that society deems acceptable, the more likely individuals may be to engage in animal cruelty and the less likely individuals and social institutions may be to seriously sanction it.

The role of gender, power, and control in animal abuse and its connection to other forms of violence is a recurrent theme in much of the research findings. Whether it is serial killers or other violent criminals who harmed animals as children or adolescents, bullies or those who have been bullied who also were cruel to animals, or batterers who threatened or hurt family pets, the abuse of animals by males to exert power and control over both humans and animals is a phenomenon that needs further understanding.

Stronger evidence is needed for the thesis that individuals graduate or progress from abusing animals to committing violence against people. Certainly, a compelling theoretical argument for this connection can be made. However, to establish support for the link more definitively, researchers will need to employ longitudinal studies and nonclinical samples.

Finally, what if researchers did not limit their investigation of the link to just illegal violence toward animals? Or to violence committed by individuals or small groups? In other words, what if scholars widened the scope of their investigation to include all forms of violence toward animals—legal and illegal, socially acceptable and unacceptable? That is, they adopted Agnew's more inclusive definition of animal abuse. What kinds of questions would this approach lead researchers to ask? At the individual level one might ask the following questions: Are hunters more likely than nonhunters to abuse their intimate partners, commit sexual assault, and/ or harm their children or pets? Are slaughterhouse employees more likely than workers in nonviolent industries to commit acts of violence against humans and other animals?

It is important not to stop at the individual level, however, but to examine the connections between institutionalized violence against animals and criminality. In a powerful critique that incorporates these issues, Beirne (2004, p. 54) argues that

> the field of human–animal studies has no scientific warrant to deploy societal definitions of acceptable and unacceptable behavior—these often are anthropocentric, arbitrary, and capricious. . . . The link between animal abuse and interhuman violence surely must be sought not only in the personal biographies of those individuals who abuse or neglect animals but also in those institutionalized social practices where animal abuse is routine, widespread, and often defined as socially acceptable.

Two sociologists who have begun asking such questions are Linda Kalof and Amy Fitzgerald (2003; Fitzgerald, Kalof, and Dietz, 2009). Their work has looked at socially acceptable violence, both at the individual and institutional levels. In an earlier study, Kalof and Fitzgerald (2003) analyzed the visual representations of "trophy" animal bodies as shown in fourteen popular hunting periodicals, arguing that these depictions simultaneously celebrate and conceal the harm inflicted upon the hunted animals. In keeping with feminist explanations for male violence, they concluded that the hunting and display of trophy animals are driven not by love of nature and animals, but by ideologies of domination and patriarchy. Not surprisingly, these images, like hunting itself, were comprised almost exclusively of white males:

> There was compelling evidence of the marginalization of animals and their bodies in the elaborate trophy exhibitions, corroborating Berger's (1980) argument that theatrical displays and animal spectacles demonstrate the absolute marginalization of animals. And consistent with the dominant hunting ideology, the covers of the magazines in our sample usually displayed images of vibrant, beautiful alive animals running gracefully through the woods, standing watchfully in the fields, eating bark from a tree, or howling on a mountaintop. But the pages between the covers were littered with dead animals, conveying an oppositional hunting discourse—the marginalization of animal bodies and the celebration of killing for trophy body parts (Kalof and Fitzgerald, 2003, p. 121).

More recently, in a truly groundbreaking study, Fitzgerald, Kalof, and Dietz (2009) investigated the link between socially accepted, institutionalized animal abuse and human crime. Using a sophisticated panel analysis of 1994–2002 data from 581 nonmetropolitan counties in states with "right to work" laws, these researchers examined the impact of slaughter-house employment, compared to that of other industries, on a community's crime rate. Specifically, they asked, Is the violent work of the "meatpacking industry" associated with increased crime rates?

To answer this question, slaughterhouses were compared with other industries, which included iron and steel forging, truck-trailer manufacturing, motor vehicle–metal stamping, sign manufacturing, and industrial launderers. The research-ers also controlled for other factors that prior research and theory had identified as explaining a community's increased crime rate: the demographic characteristics of workers, increased unemployment rates, and social disorganization in the community. The following variables served as controls in the analysis: the number of males in the community ages fifteen to thirty-four, population density, the total number of males, the number living in poverty, international migration, internal migration, total nonwhite population, and the unem-ployment rate.

As hypothesized, slaughterhouse employment was signifi-cantly related to higher crime rates as well as report rates. Slaughterhouse employment, compared to other industries, increased total arrest rates for violent crimes, rape, and other sex offenses. Specifically, for every additional slaughterhouse worker, the arrest rate went up by .013 arrests. According to Fitzgerald et al., an average-sized slaughterhouse—one with 175 employees—led to an increase in the arrest scale by 2.224 arrests and in the report scale by 4.69 reports. To further put the findings in perspective, the expected arrest and report val-ues in counties with 7,500 employees were more than double the values where there were no slaughterhouse employees. This is the first study documenting a link between institutionalized animal abuse and increased crime. We can hope that others investigating similar relationships will follow.

Questions for Discussion

1. How should the law view companion animals when it comes to issues of divorce and custody, and family violence?
2. What services do you think shelters should provide for battered women with pets?
3. Evaluate Agnew's definition of animal abuse. Do you like it? Why or why not?

7

Expanding the Sociological Imagination

An Inclusive Sociology of Animal Abuse

Increasingly, scholars are recognizing that research on animal abuse has been anthropocentric and speciesist. By "anthropocentric" I mean that the focus of the research has been humans, with animals only considered at the periphery. By "speciesist," I mean research based on an ideology that views humans as superior to other animals, leading to the favoring of human interests over those of other animals and, thus, to animal exploitation. This is true in at least three significant and interrelated ways.

First, animal abuse has been typically conceptualized by researchers as a sign of psychopathology. Second, research on animal abuse, unlike other forms of violence, has been motivated almost exclusively by its association with violence against humans, rather than being seen as worthy of academic investigation in its own right (Cazaux, 1998; Solot, 1997). Consequently, in both cases, animals are not examined as central participants of the interactions, and their abuse is not the focus of the inquiry. So the abuse of animals was seen as evidence of mental illness, as a predictor of subsequent violence against humans, or as another form of wife (or child) abuse. As Beirne (1999, p. 140) has stated, "[P]erhaps society will eventually reach the conclusion that animal abuse should be censured not because it is similar to the abuse of humans but because it is loathsome to animals themselves."

Third, research has focused on violence toward animals that is defined as socially unacceptable, unnecessary, and illegal actions committed by individuals. Such an approach excludes from consideration legal forms of violence committed both by individuals (e.g., hunting) and institutionalized violence (e.g., factory farming and animal experimentation) that account for the vast majority of the harm inflicted upon nonhuman animals (Agnew, 1998; Beirne, 1999; 2004). By linking the definition of animal abuse to prevailing beliefs about animals, beliefs that are social constructions that vary by time and place, "[W]e let those political and social actors with the greatest power determine our definition of animal abuse" (Agnew, 1998, p. 180).

Some criminologists have already begun to approach the study of animal abuse from a perspective that is less anthropocentric and speciesist (Agnew, 1998; Beirne, 1997, 1999, 2009; Cazaux, 1998, 1999). Agnew's (1998) social-psychological theory of animal abuse discussed in chapter 5 is an excellent example. Additionally, Beirne (1999) has argued persuasively for a "nonspeciesist criminology," in which animal abuse is recognized as a legitimate subject for research, irrespective of its relationship to interhuman violence. In an earlier article, Beirne (1997) applied a nonspeciesist approach to the analysis of bestiality. He argued that because human–animal sexual relations shared certain key features with sexual assaults against women and children—namely, they are coercive, painful (and sometimes deadly), and animals are unable to give their consent or report their abuse—such relations should also be illegal. Recognizing the parallels between the sexual assault of animals and that of women and children initially led Beirne to propose replacing the anthropocentric term "bestiality" with the term "interspecies sexual assault," which he has subsequently replaced with the simpler, more straightforward "animal sexual assault" (Beirne, 2009).

These innovative approaches point the way to a more inclusive sociology of animal abuse, where other animals are seen as worthy of moral consideration, and whose victimization, like that of other disadvantaged groups—including women, racial/ethnic minorities, and the poor—is seen not just as individual and pathological, but as systemic and institutional. Sociology, which has a rich and proud history of exposing and challenging oppression and inequality based on gender, race, class, age, and sexual orientation, must now widen its scope to include other animals in its sphere of study, and to include speciesism in its rightful place alongside other forms of oppression.

CONCLUSIONS

Over three decades ago, Bryant issued a challenge to his colleagues in sociology to incorporate other animals in their sphere of inquiry. In particular, Bryant argued that it was in the area he called "zoological crime"—crime, delinquency, and deviancy involving animals—that researchers would likely "encounter the most fertile phenomenological fields to plow" (Bryant, 1979, p. 412). Animal abuse—whether as a marker of violence in families, a precursor or indicator of other forms of criminality, or as an act of violence against innocent nonhuman victims—provides an excellent opportunity in sociology, criminology, social work, and other related fields for empirical investigation, theory development, and the practical application of research findings to social policy. And as a result, the fruit of this scholarly labor may contribute to a world that is safer and less violent for all of its inhabitants—human and animal alike.

Questions for Discussion

1. How has research on animal abuse been anthropocentric and speciesist?
2. Propose a study examining violence to animals that would not be anthropocentric and speciesist.
3. In what ways is the exploitation of other animals similar to the exploitation of other human groups—such as women, racial/ethnic minorities, and the poor? In what ways is it different?

Adams, Carol J. 1994. "Bringing Peace Home: A Feminist Philosophical Perspective on the Abuse of Women, Children, and Pet Animals." *Hypatia* 9:63–84.

_____. 1995. "Woman-battering and Harm to Animals." In *Animals and Women: Feminist Theoretical Explorations*, edited by Carol J. Adams and Josephine Donovan (pp. 55–84). Durham, N.C.: Duke University Press.

Agnew, Robert. 1998. "The Causes of Animal Abuse: A Social-Psychological Analysis." *Theoretical Criminology* 2:177–209.

Albert, Alexa, and Kris Bulcroft. 1988. "Pets, Families, and the Life Course." *Journal of Marriage and the Family* 50:543–52.

Alger, Janet M., and Steven F. Alger. 1997. "Beyond Mead: Symbolic Interaction between Humans and Felines." *Society & Animals* 5:65–81.

_____. 1999. "Cat Culture, Human Culture: An Ethnographic Study of a Cat Shelter." *Society & Animals* 7:199–218.

Alys, Llian, J. Claire Wilson, John Clarke, and Peter Toman. 2009. "Developmental Animal Cruelty and Its Correlates in Sexual Homicide Offenders and Sex Offenders." In *The Link between Animal Abuse and Human Violence*, edited by Andrew Linzey (pp. 145–62). Eastbourne, East Sussex, U.K.: Sussex Academic Press.

American Pet Products Association. 2011. "**2011–2012 APPA National Pet Owners Survey**," retrieved at www.americanpetproducts.org/press_industrytrends.asp.

Animal Legal Defense Fund. 2011. "U.S. Jurisdictions with and without Felony Animal Cruelty Provisions," retrieved at www.aldf.org/article.php?id=261.

Arkow, Phil. 1999. "The Evolution of Animal Welfare as a Human Welfare Concern." In *Child Abuse, Domestic Violence, and Animal Abuse: Linking the Circles of Compassion for Prevention and Intervention*, edited by Frank R. Ascione and Phil Arkow (pp. 19–37). West Lafayette, Ind.: Purdue University Press.

_____. 2011, July. "Connecticut Enacts Landmark Cross-Reporting Law." *The LINK-Letter*, National Link Coalition, retrieved at www.nationlinkcoalition.org.

Arluke, Arnold. 2002. "Animal Abuse as Dirty Play." *Symbolic Interaction* 2:405–430.

_____. 2004. *Brute Force: Animal Police and the Challenge of Cruelty*. West Lafayette, Ind.: Purdue University Press.

_____. 2006. *Just a Dog: Understanding Animal Cruelty and Ourselves*. Philadelphia: Temple University Press.

Arluke, Arnold, and Carter Luke. 1997. "Physical Cruelty toward Animals in Massachusetts, 1975–1996." *Society & Animals* 5:195–204.

Arluke, Arnold, and Clinton R. Sanders. 1996. *Regarding Animals*. Philadelphia: Temple University Press.

Arluke, Arnold, Jack Levin, Carter Luke, and Frank Ascione. 1999. "The Relationship of Animal Abuse to Violence and Other Forms of Antisocial Behavior." *Journal of Interpersonal Violence* 14:963–75.

Ascione, Frank R. 1993. "Children Who Are Cruel to Animals: A Review of Research and Implications for Developmental Psychology." *Anthrozoös* 6:226–47.

_____. 1998. "Battered Women's Reports of Their Partners' and Their Children's Cruelty to Animals." *Journal of Emotional Abuse* 1:119–33.

_____. 1999. "The Abuse of Animals and Human Interpersonal Violence: Making the Connection." In *Child Abuse, Domestic Violence and Animal Abuse: Linking the Circles of Compassion for Prevention and Intervention*, edited by Frank R. Ascione and Phil Arkow (pp. 50–61). West Lafayette, Ind.: Purdue University Press.

_____. 2001. "Animal Abuse and Youth Violence." *Juvenile Justice Bulletin*. Washington, D.C.: Office of Juvenile Justice.

Ascione, Frank R., and Phil Arkow. 1999. *Child Abuse, Domestic Violence and Animal Abuse: Linking the Circles of Compassion for Prevention and Intervention*. West Lafayette, Ind.: Purdue University Press.

Ascione, Frank R., and Randall Lockwood. 2001. "Cruelty to Animals: Changing Psychological, Social, and Legislative Perspectives." In *State of the Animals 2000*, edited by Deborah J. Salem and Andrew N. Rowan (pp. 39–53). Washington, D.C.: Humane Society Press.

Ascione, Frank R., and Kenneth Shapiro. 2009. "People and Animals, Kindness and Cruelty: Research Directions and Policy Implications." *Journal of Social Issues* 65:569–87.

Ascione, Frank R., Claudia V. Weber, and David S. Wood. 1997. "The Abuse of Animals and Domestic Violence: A National Survey of Shelters for Women Who Are Battered." *Society & Animals* 5:205–18.

Ascione, Frank R., William N. Friedrich, John Heath, and Kentaro Hayashi. 2003. "Cruelty to Animals in Normative, Sexually Abused, and Outpatient Psychiatric Samples of 6- to 12-Year-Old Children: Relations to Maltreatment and Exposure to Domestic Violence." *Anthrozoös* 16:194–212.

Ascione, Frank R., Claudia V. Weber, Teresa M. Thompson, John Heath, Mike Maruyama, and Kentaro Hayashi. 2007. "Battered Pets and Domestic Violence: Animal Abuse Reported by Women Experiencing Intimate Violence and by Non-Abused Women." *Violence Against Women* 13:354–73.

Baldry, Anna C. 2003. "Animal Abuse and Exposure to Interparental Violence in Italian Youth." *Journal of Interpersonal Violence* 18:258–81.

———. 2004. "The Development of the P.E.T. Scale for the Measurement of Physical and Emotional Tormenting Against Animals in Adolescents." *Society & Animals* 12:1–17.

———. 2005. "Animal Abuse among Preadolescents Directly and Indirectly Victimized at School and at Home." *Criminal Behaviour & Mental Health* 15:97–110.

Baron, Larry, and Murray A. Straus. 1988. "Cultural and Economic Sources of Homicide in the United States." *Sociological Quarterly* 29:371–90.

Beirne, Piers. 1997. "Rethinking Bestiality: Towards a Concept of Interspecies Sexual Assault." *Theoretical Criminology* 1:317–40.

———. 1999. "For a Nonspeciesist Criminology: Animal Abuse as an Object of Study." *Criminology* 37:117–47.

———. 2004. "From Animal Abuse to Interhuman Violence?

A Critical Review of the Progression Thesis." *Society & Animals* 12:39–65.

_____. 2009. *Confronting Animal Abuse: Law, Criminology, and Human–Animal Relationships*. Lanham, Md.: Rowman & Littlefield.

Blumer, Herbert. 1969. *Symbolic Interactionism: Perspective and Method*. Englewood Cliffs, N.J.: Prentice-Hall.

Boat, Barbara W. 1995. "The Relationship between Violence to Children and Violence to Animals: An Ignored Link?" *Journal of Interpersonal Violence* 10:229–35.

Bodsworth, Wendie, and G. J. Coleman. 2001. "Child–Companion Animal Attachment in Single and Two-Parent Families." *Anthrozoös* 14:216–23.

Bogdon, Robert, and Steven J. Taylor. 1989. "Relationships with Severely Disabled People: The Social Construction of Humanness." *Social Problems* 36:135–48.

Bowd, Alan D., and Anne C. Bowd. 1989. "Attitudes toward the Treatment of Animals: A Study of Christian Groups in Australia." *Anthrozoös* 3:20–24.

Brennan, Sharon. 2007. "Animals as Disregarded Pawns in Family Violence: Exclusionary Practices of Feminists Based Refuge Policies." *Electronic Journal of Sociology*, retrieved at www.sociology.org/content/2007/__brennan_pawns.pdf.

Browne, Angela. 1987. *When Battered Women Kill*. New York: Free Press.

Bryant, Clifton D. 1979. "The Zoological Connection: Animal-Related Human Behavior." *Social Forces* 58:399–421.

Cain, Ann. 1983. "A Study of Pets in the Family System."

In , edited by Aaron. H. Katcher and Alan M. Beck (pp. 72–81). Philadelphia: University of Pennsylvania Press.

Carlisle-Frank, Pamela, and Joshua M. Frank. 2006. "Owners, Guardians, and Owner-Guardians: Differing Relationship with Pets." *Anthrozoös* 19:225–42.

Cazaux, Geertrui. 1998. "Legitimating the Entry of 'The Animals Issue' Into (Critical) Criminology." *Humanity and Society* 22:365–85.

_____. 1999. "Beauty and the Beast: Animal Abuse from a Non-speciesist Criminological Perspective." *Law & Social Change* 31:105–126.

Cohen, Susan P. 2002. "Can Pets Function as Family Members?" *Western Journal of Nursing Research* 24:621–38.

Coston, Charisse, and Babette M. Protz. 1998. "Kill Your Dog, Beat Your Wife, Screw Your Neighbor's Kids, Rob a Bank? A Cursory Look at an Individual's Vat of Social Chaos Resulting from Deviance." 26:153–58.

Dadds, Mark R., Clare Whiting, Paul Bunin, Jennifer A. Fraser, Juliana H. Charlson, and Andrew Pirola-Merlo. 2004. "Measurement of Cruelty in Children: The Cruelty to Animals Inventory." *Journal of Abnormal Child Psychology* 32:321–34.

Darden, Donna K., and Steven K. Worden. 1996. "Marketing Deviance: The Selling of Cockfighting." *Society & Animals* 4:211–31.

DeGue, Sarah, and David DeLillo. 2009. "Is Animal Cruelty a 'Red Flag' for Family Violence? Investigating Co-occurring Violence toward Children, Partners, and Pets." *Journal of Interpersonal Violence* 24:1036–56.

DeViney, Elizabeth, Jeffery Dickert, and Randall Lockwood.

1983. "The Care of Pets within Child Abusing Families." *International Journal for the Study of Animal Problems* 4:321–29.

Dutton, Mary A. 1992. *Empowering and Healing the Battered Woman.* New York: Springer.

Faller, Kathleen C. 1990. *Understanding Child Sexual Maltreatment.* Newbury Park, Calif.: Sage.

Faver, Catherine A., and A. M. Cavazos, Jr. 2007. "Animal Abuse and Domestic Violence: A View from the Border." *Journal of Emotional Abuse* 7:59–81.

Faver, Catherine A., and Elizabeth B. Strand. 2003. "To Leave or to Stay? Battered Women's Concern for Vulnerable Pets." *Journal of Interpersonal Violence* 18:1367–1377.

———. 2007. "Fear, Guilt, and Grief: Harm to Pets and the Emotional Abuse of Women." *Journal of Emotional Abuse* 7:51–70.

———. 2008. "Unleashing Compassion: Social Work and Animal Abuse." In *International Handbook of Animal Abuse and Cruelty: Theory, Research, and Application*, edited by Frank R. Ascione (pp. 175–99). West Lafayette, Ind.: Purdue University Press.

Felthous, Alan R., and Stephen R. Kellert. 1986. "Violence against Animals and People: Is Aggression against Living Creatures Generalized?" *Bulletin of the American Academy of Psychiatry Law* 14:55–69.

———. 1987. "Psychosocial Aspects of Selecting Animal Species for Physical Abuse." *Journal of Forensic Sciences* 32:1713–1723.

Fine, Gary A. 1986. "The Dirty Play of Little Boys." *Society* 24:63–67.

Finkelhor, David, Linda M. Williams, and Nanci Burns. 1988. *Nursery Crimes: Sexual Abuse in Day Care.* Newbury Park, Calif.: Sage.

Fitzgerald, Amy J. 2005. *Animal Abuse and Family Violence: Researching the Interrelationships of Abusive Power.* Edwin Mellen Press, Mellen Studies in Sociology.

_____. 2007. "'They Gave Me a Reason to Live': The Protective Effects of Companion Animals on the Suicidality of Abused Women." *Humanity and Society* 31:355–378.

Fitzgerald, Amy, Linda Kalof, and Thomas Dietz. 2009. "Slaughterhouses and Increased Crime Rates: An Empirical Analysis of the Spillover from 'The Jungle' into the Surrounding Community." *Organization & Environment* 22:158–84.

Flynn, Clifton P. 1999a. "Animal Abuse in Childhood and Later Support for Interpersonal Violence in Families." *Society & Animals* 7:161–72.

_____. 1999b. "Exploring the Link between Corporal Punishment and Children's Cruelty to Animals." *Journal of Marriage and the Family* 61:971–81.

_____. 2000a. "Battered Women and Their Animal Companions: Symbolic Interaction between Human and Nonhuman Animals." *Society & Animals* 8:99–127.

_____. 2000b. "Why Family Professionals Can No Longer Ignore Violence toward Animals." *Family Relations* 49:87–95.

_____. 2000c. "Woman's Best Friend: Pet Abuse and the Role of Companion Animals in the Lives of Battered Women." *Violence Against Women* 6:162–77.

_____. 2001. "Acknowledging the 'Zoological Connection':

A Sociological Analysis of Animal Cruelty." *Society &*
Animals 9:71–87.

_____. 2008. "A Sociological Analysis of Animal Abuse." In
International Handbook of Animal Abuse and Cruelty: The-
ory, Research, and Application, edited by Frank R. Ascione
(pp. 155–74). West Lafayette, Ind.: Purdue University Press.

_____. 2009. "Women-battering, Pet Abuse, and Human–Ani-
mal Relationships." In *The Link between Animal Abuse*
and Human Violence, edited by Andrew Linzey (pp. 116–
25). Eastbourne, East Sussex, U.K.: Sussex Academic Press.

_____. 2011. "Examining the Links between Animal Abuse
and Human Violence." *Crime, Law and Social Change*
55:453–68.

Forsythe, Craig J., and Rhonda D. Evans. 1998. "Dogmen:
The Rationalization of Deviance." *Society& Animals*
6:203–18.

Francione, Gary L. 1996. *Rain without Thunder: The Ideol-*
ogy of the Animal Rights Movement. Philadelphia: Temple University Press.

Gelles, Richard J. 1993. "Through a Sociological Lens: Social
Structure and Family Violence." In *Current Controversies*
on Family Violence, edited by Richard Gelles and Donileen
Loseke (pp. 31–46). Newbury Park, Calif.: Sage.

_____. 1997. *Intimate Violence in Families, 3rd. edition*.
Thousand Oaks, Calif.: Sage.

Gelles, Richard J., and Murray A. Straus. 1979. "Determi-
nants of Violence in the Family: Toward a Theoretical
Integration." In *Contemporary Theories about the Family*,
vol.1, edited by R. Burr, R. Hill, F. I. Nye, and I. L. Reiss
(pp. 549–81). New York: Free Press.

_____. 1988. *Intimate Violence*. New York: Simon and Schuster.

Gleyzer, Roman, Alan R. Felthous, and Charles E. Holzer. 2002. "Animal Cruelty and Psychiatric Disorders." *Journal of the American Academy of Psychiatry and the Law* 30:257–65.

Gullone, Eleanora, and Nerida Robertson. 2008. "The Relationship between Bullying and Animal Abuse Behaviors in Adolescents: The Importance of Witnessing Animal Abuse." *Journal of Applied Developmental Psychology* 29:371–79.

Guymer, Elise C., David Mellor, Ernest S. L. Luk, and Vicky Pearse. 2001. "The Development of a Screening Questionnaire for Childhood Cruelty to Animals." *Journal of Child Psychology and Psychiatry* 42:1057–63.

Hawley, Fred. 1993. "The Moral and Conceptual Universe of Cockfighters: Symbolism and Rationalization." *Society & Animals* 1:159–68.

Henry, Bill C. 2004a. "Exposure to Animal Abuse and Group Context: Two Factors Affecting Participation in Animal Abuse." *Anthrozoös* 17:290–305.

_____. 2004b. "The Relationship between Animal Cruelty, Delinquency, and Attitudes toward the Treatment of Nonhuman Animals." *Society & Animals* 12:185–207.

Henry, Bill C., and Cheryl E. Sanders. 2007. "Bullying and Animal Abuse: Is There a Connection?" *Society & Animals* 15:107–26.

Hensley, Christopher, and Suzanne E. Tallichet. 2009. "Childhood and Adolescent Animal Cruelty Methods and Their Possible Link to Adult Violent Crimes." *Journal of Interpersonal Violence* 24:147–58.

Hensley, Christopher, Suzanne E. Tallichet, and Erik L. Dut-kiewicz. 2009. "Recurrent Childhood Animal Cruelty: Is There a Relationship to Adult Recurrent Interpersonal Violence?" *Criminal Justice Review* 34:248–57.

Herzog, Harold A., Nancy S. Betchart, and Robert B. Pittman. 1991. "Gender, Sex Role Orientation, and Attitudes toward Animals." *Anthrozoös* 4:184–91.

Humane Society of the United States. 2011. "State Animal Cruelty Chart, April. 2011." Retrieved at www.humanesociety.org/assets/pdfs/abuse/state_animal_cruelty_laws_11.pdf.

Irvine, Leslie. 2004. *If You Tame Me: Understanding Our Connection with Animals.* Philadelphia: Temple University Press.

Jory, Brian, and Mary Lou Randour. 1999. *The AniCare Model of Treatment for Animal Abuse.* Washington Grove, Md.: Psychologists for the Ethical Treatment of Animals.

Kalof, Linda, and Amy Fitzgerald. 2003. "Reading the Trophy: Exploring the Display of Dead Animals in Hunting Magazines." *Visual Studies* 18:112–22.

Kellert, Stephen R., and Alan R. Felthous. 1985. "Childhood Cruelty toward Animals among Criminals and Non-criminals." *Human Relations* 38:1113–29.

Kelley, Harold, Ellen Berscheid, Andrew Christensen, John Harvey, Ted Huston, George Levinger, Evie McClinton, Letitia A. Peplau, and Donald Peterson. 1983. *Close Relationships.* New York: W. H. Freeman.

Kogan, Lori R., Sherry McConnell, Regina Schoenfeld-Tacher, and Pia Jansen-Lock. 2004. "Crosstrails: A Unique

Foster Program to Provide Safety for Pets of Women in Safehouses." *Violence Against Women* 10:418–34.

Kruse, Corwin R. 2002. "Baby Steps: Minnesota Raises Certain Forms of Animal Cruelty to Felony Status." *William Mitchell Law Review* 28:1649–80.

Lacroix, Charlotte A. 1999. "Another Weapon for Combating Family Violence: Prevention of Animal Abuse." In *Child Abuse, Domestic Violence, and Animal Abuse: Linking the Circles of Compassion for Prevention and Intervention*, edited by Frank R. Ascione and Phil Arkow (pp. 62–80). West Lafayette, Ind.: Purdue University Press.

Levin, Jack, and Arnold Arluke. 2009. "Reducing the Link's False Positive Problem." In *The Link between Animal Abuse and Human* Violence, edited by Andrew Linzey (pp. 163–71). Eastbourne, East Sussex, U.K.: Sussex Academic Press.

Lockwood, Randall, and Frank R. Ascione. 1998. *Cruelty to Animals and Interpersonal Violence: Readings in Research and Application*. West Lafayette, Ind.: Purdue University Press.

Loring, Marti T., and Tamara A. Bolden-Hines. 2004. "Pet Abuse by Batterers as a Means of Coercing Battered Women into Committing Illegal Behavior." *Journal of Emotional Abuse* 4:27–37.

Luk, Ernset S. L., Petra K. Staiger, Lisa Wong, and John Mathai. 1999." Children Who Are Cruel to Animals: A Revisit." *Australian and New Zealand Journal of Psychiatry* 33:29–36.

Mead, George H. 1934. *Mind, Self, and Society.* Chicago: University of Chicago Press.

Merz-Perez, Linda, and Kathleen M. Heide. 2004. *Animal*

Cruelty: Pathway to Violence against People. Walnut Creek, Calif.: AltaMira Press.

Merz-Perez, Linda, Kathleen M. Heide, and Ira J. Silverman. 2001. "Childhood Cruelty to Animals and Subsequent Violence against Humans." *International Journal of Offender Therapy and Comparative Criminology* 25:556–73.

Miller, Karla S., and John F. Knutson. 1997. "Reports of Severe Physical Punishment and Exposure to Animal Cruelty by Inmates Convicted of Felonies and by University Students." *Child Abuse and Neglect* 21:59–82.

Munro, Helen M. C. 1999. "The Battered Pet: Signs and Symptoms." In *Child Abuse, Domestic Violence, and Animal Abuse: Linking the Circles of Compassion for Prevention and Intervention*, edited by Frank R. Ascione and Phil Arkow (pp. 199–208). West Lafayette, Ind.: Purdue University Press.

Owens, David J., and Murray A. Straus. 1975. "The Social Structure of Violence in Childhood and Approval of Violence as an Adult." *Aggressive Behavior* 1:193–211.

Pagani, Camilla, Francesco Robustelli, and Frank R. Ascione. 2010. "Investigating Animal Abuse: Some Theoretical and Methodological Issues." *Anthrozoös* 23:259–76.

Patronek, Gary. 1996. "Hoarding of Animals: An Under-recognized Public Health Problem in a Difficult to Study Population." *Public Health Reports* 114:82–87.

———. 2008. "Animal Hoarding: A Third Dimension of Animal Abuse." In *International Handbook of Animal Abuse and Cruelty: Theory, Research, and Application*, edited by Frank R. Acsione (pp. 221-240). West Lafayette, Ind.: Purdue University Press.

Patterson-Kane, Emily G., and Heather Piper. 2009. "Animal

Abuse as a Sentinel for Human Violence: A Critique." *Journal of Social Issues* 65:589–614.

Peek, Charles W., Nancy J. Bell, and Charlotte C. Dunham. 1996. "Gender, Gender Ideology, and Animal Rights Advocacy." *Gender & Society* 10:464–78.

Pifer, Linda K. 1996. "Exploring the Gender Gap in Young Adults' Attitudes about Animal Research." *Society and Animals* 4:37–52.

Piper, Heather. 2003. "The Linkage of Animal Abuse with Interpersonal Violence: A Sheep in Wolf's Clothing?" *Journal of Social Work* 3:161–77.

Randour, Mary Lou, and Tio Hardiman. 2007. "Creating Synergy: Taking a Look at Animal Fighting and Gangs." *Proceedings of The Hamilton Fish Institute*, sponsored by the Office of Juvenile Justice and Delinquency Prevention, U. S. Department of Justice, Washington, D.C.

Randour, Mary Lou, Susan Krinsk, and Joanne Wolf. 2002. *AniCare Child: An Assessment and Treatment Approach for Childhood Animal Abuse*. Washington Grove, Md.: Psychologists for the Ethical Treatment of Animals.

Renzetti, Claire M. 1992. *Violent Betrayal: Partner Abuse in Lesbian Relationships*. Newbury Park, Calif.: Sage Publications.

Ressler, Robert K., Ann W. Burgess, Carol R. Hartman, John E. Douglas, and Arlene McCormack. 1986. "Murderers Who Rape and Mutilate." *Journal of Interpersonal Violence* 1:273–87.

Rigdon, John D., and Tapia, Fernando. 1977. "Children Who Are Cruel to Animals—A Follow-up Study." *Journal of Operational Psychiatry* 8:27–36.

Rowan, Andrew. 1992. "The Dark Side of the 'Force.'" *Anthrozoös* 5:4–5.

Sanders, Clinton R. 1993. "Understanding Dogs: Caretakers' Attributions of Mindedness in Canine–Human Relationships." *Journal of Contemporary Ethnography* 22:205–26.

_____. 1999. *Understanding Dogs: Living and Working with Canine Companions*. Philadelphia: Temple University Press.

Siegel, Judith M. 1993. "Companion Animals: In Sickness and in Health." *Journal of Social Issues* 49:157–67.

Simmons, Catherine A., and Peter Lehmann. 2007. "Exploring the Link between Pet Abuse and Controlling Behaviors in Violent Relationships." *Journal of Interpersonal Violence* 22:1211–22.

Singer, Peter. 1990. *Animal Liberation*. New York: Avon Books.

Solot, Dorian. 1997. "Untangling the Animal Abuse Web." *Society and Animals* 5:257–65.

Spelman, E. V. 1982. "Woman as Body: Ancient and Contemporary Views." *Feminist Studies* 8:109–31.

Strand, Elizabeth B., and Catherine A. Faver. 2005. "Battered Women's Concern for their Pets: A Closer Look." *Journal of Family Social Work* 9:39–58.

Straus, Murray A. 1980. "A Sociological Perspective on the Causes of Family Violence." In *Violence and the Family*, edited by M. R. Green (pp. 7–31). Boulder, Colo.: Westview.

_____. 1991. "Discipline and Deviance: Physical Punishment of Children and Violence and Other Crime in Adulthood." *Social Problems* 38:133–54.

_____. 1994. *Beating the Devil Out of Them: Corporal Punishment in American Families*. New York: Lexington Books.

Straus, Murray A., Richard J. Gelles, and Suzanne K. Steinmetz. 1980. *Behind Closed Doors*. New York: Doubleday/Anchor.

Sykes, Gresham M., and David Matza. 1957. "Techniques of Neutralization: A Theory of Delinquency." *American Sociological Review* 22:664–70.

Tallichet, Suzanne E., and Christopher Hensley. 2004. "Exploring the Link between Recurrent Acts of Childhood and Adolescent Animal Cruelty and Subsequent Violent Crime." *Criminal Justice Review* 29:304–16.

Tallichet, Suzanne E., Christopher Hensley, and Stephen D. Singer. 2005. "Unraveling the Methods of Childhood and Adolescent Cruelty to Non-human Animals." *Society & Animals* 13:91–108.

Tapia, Fernando. 1971. "Children Who Are Cruel to Animals." *Child Psychiatry and Human Development* 2:70–77.

Thompson, Kelly L., and Eleanora Gullone. 2006. "An Investigation into the Association between the Witnessing of Animal Abuse and Adolescents' Behavior toward Animals." *Society & Animals* 14:221–43.

Tingle, David, George W. Barnard, Lynn Robbins, Gustave Newman, and David Hutchinson. 1986. "Childhood and Adolescent Characteristics of Pedophiles and Rapists." *International Journal of Law and Psychiatry* 9:103–116.

U.S. Census Bureau. 2006. "Table 1: Resident Population by Age and Sex: 1980–2004." Statistical abstract of the United States, retrieved at www.census.gov/ prod/2005pubs/06statab/pop.pdf.

Vaughn, Michael G., Qiang Fu, Matt DeLisi, Kevin M. Beaver, Brian E. Perron, Katie Terrell, and Matthew O. Howard. 2009. "Correlates of Cruelty to Animals in the United States: Results from the National Epidemiologic Survey on Alcohol and Related Conditions." *Journal of Psychiatric Research* 43:1213–18.

Veevers, Jean E. 1985. "The Social Meanings of Pets: Alternative Roles for Companion Animals." *Marriage and Family Review* 8:11–30.

Verlinden, Stephanie, Michel Hersen, and Jay Thomas. 2001. "Risk Factors in School Shootings." *Clinical Psychology Review* 20:3–56.

Vermeulen, Hannelie, and Johannes S. J. Odendaal. 1993. "Proposed Typology of Companion Animal Abuse." *Anthrozoös* 6:248–57.

Volant, Anne M., Judy A. Johnson, Eleanora Gullone, and Grahame J. Coleman. 2008. "The Relationship between Domestic Violence and Animal Abuse." *Journal of Interpersonal Violence* 23:1277–95.

Walker, Lenore E. 1979. *The Battered Woman.* New York: Harper and Row.

Walsh, Froma. 2009. "Human–Animal Bonds II: The Role of Pets in Family Systems and Family Therapy." *Family Process* 48:481–99.

Walton-Moss, Benita J., Jennifer Manganello, Victoria Frye, and Jacquelyn C. Campbell. 2005. "Risk Factors for Intimate Partner Violence and Associated Injury among Urban Women." *Journal of Community Health* 30:377–89.

Wiehe, Vernon R. 1990. *Sibling Abuse*. New York: Lexington Books.

Wisch, Rebecca F. 2011. "Domestic Violence and Pets: List of States that Include Pets in Protection Orders." Animal Legal and Historical Center, Michigan State University College of Law. Retrieved at www.animallaw.info/articles/ovusdomesticviolencelaws.htm.

Wright, Jeremy, and Christopher Hensley. 2003. "From Animal Cruelty to Serial Murder: Applying the Graduation Hypothesis." *International Journal of Offender Therapy and Comparative Criminology* 47:71–88.

Yllo, Kersti 1993. "Through a Feminist Lens: Gender, Power, and Violence." In *Current Controversies on Family Violence*, edited by Richard Gelles and Donileen Loseke (pp. 47–62). Newbury Park, Calif.: Sage.

Zilney, Lisa A. and Zilney, Mary. 2005. "Reunification of Child and Animal Welfare Agencies: Cross-reporting of Abuse in Wellington County, Ontario." *Child Welfare* 84:47–66.

ABOUT THE AUTHOR

Clifton P. Flynn, PhD, is professor of sociology and chair of the Department of Sociology, Criminal Justice, and Women's Studies at the University of South Carolina Upstate. He is a past chair of the Section on Animals and Society of the American Sociological Association. Dr. Flynn serves on the editorial boards of *Society & Animals* and the *Journal of Animal Ethics*, and served from 2005 to 2010 on the editorial board of *Anthrozoös*. In 2008, he was selected as a fellow of the Oxford Centre for Animal Ethics. Dr. Flynn is also a fellow of the Institute for Human–Animal Connection at the University of Denver's Graduate School of Social Work. His Animals and Society course was chosen as the "Best New Animals and Society Course" by the Humane Society of the United States in 2001. He is also the editor of *Social Creatures*, one of the first anthologies in Human–Animal Studies (Lantern Books, 2008).

ABOUT THE PUBLISHER

LANTERN PUBLISHING & MEDIA was founded in 2020 to follow and expand on the legacy of Lantern Books—a publishing company started in 1999 on the principles of living with a greater depth and commitment to the preservation of the natural world. Like its predecessor, Lantern Publishing & Media produces books on animal advocacy, veganism, religion, social justice, and psychology and family therapy. Lantern is dedicated to printing in the United States on recycled paper and saving resources in our day-to-day operations. Our titles are also available as ebooks and audiobooks.

To catch up on Lantern's publishing program, visit us at www. lanternpm.org.

facebook.com/lanternpm
instagram.com/lanternpm
twitter.com/lanternpm